About this Book

An Introduction to Windows Vista was written for you if you have bought a new PC in the last few years with Windows Vista as its operating system. Vista manages the available resources of a computer and 'controls' the programs that run on it. To get the most from your computer it is important that you have a good working knowledge of Vista.

The book is produced in full colour and covers the Vista environment with its many windows. It explains as simply as possible: how to organise your files, folders and photos; how to use Internet Explorer for your Web browsing and Microsoft Mail for your e-mails; how to control your PC and keep it healthy; and how to use Vista's Accessibility features if you have poor eyesight or have problems using the keyboard or mouse.

The material in the book is presented using everyday language, avoiding jargon as much as possible. It was written with the non technical, non computer literate person in mind. It is hoped that with its help you will be able to get the most out of your computer, when using Windows Vista, and that you will be able to do it in the shortest, most effective and enjoyable way. Most of all, have fun!

About the Authors

Phil Oliver graduated in Mining Engineering at Camborne School of Mines and has specialised in most aspects of surface mining technology, with a particular emphasis on computer related techniques. He has worked in Guyana, Canada, several Middle Eastern and Central Asian countries, South Africa and the United Kingdom, on such diverse projects as: the planning and management of bauxite, iron, gold and coal mines; rock excavation contracting in the UK; international mining equipment sales and international mine consulting. He later took up a lecturing position at Camborne School of Mines (part of Exeter University) in Surface Mining and Management. He has now retired, to spend more time writing (www.philoliver.com) and developing Web sites.

Noel Kantaris graduated in Electrical Engineering at Bristol University and after spending three years in the Electronics Industry in London, took up a Tutorship in Physics at the University of Queensland. Research interests in Ionospheric Physics, led to the degrees of M.E. in Electronics and Ph.D. in Physics. On return to the UK, he took up a Post-Doctoral Research Fellowship in Radio Physics at the University of Leicester, and then a lecturing position in Engineering at the Camborne School of Mines, Cornwall, (part of Exeter University), where he was also the CSM Computing Manager. At present he is IT Director of FFC Ltd.

Trademarks

Microsoft, **Windows**, **Windows Aero**, **Windows XP**, and **Windows Vista** are either registered trademarks or trademarks of Microsoft Corporation.

All other brand and product names used in the book are recognised as trademarks, or registered trademarks, of their respective companies.

Contents

Using the Windows Key

Using the Windows key ⊞ with the following keyboard shortcuts gives you very quick access to many of Vista's features. These are well worth learning as they will save you a lot of time.

⊞	Open or close the **Start** menu.
⊞+*n*	Open the *nth* program on the **Quick Launch** bar.
⊞+Break	Opens the **System Properties** box.
⊞+B	Move focus to the **Notification** area.
⊞+D	Toggle showing the Desktop.
⊞+E	Open **Computer** window.
⊞+F	Search for a file or folder.
⊞+L	Lock your computer.
⊞+M	Minimise all windows to the Taskbar.
⊞+Shift+M	Restore minimised windows to the Desktop.
⊞+R	Open the **Run** box.
⊞+T	Cycle through programs on the Taskbar.
⊞+Tab	Cycle through programs on the Taskbar using Vista's **Flip 3-D**.
⊞+Space	Move focus to the **Sidebar**.
⊞+G	Cycle through **Sidebar** gadgets.
⊞+U	Open the **Ease of Access Center**.
⊞+X	Open the **Windows Mobility Center**.

1

A First Look at Vista

Windows Vista is an Operating System for PCs which is produced by Microsoft. It is the software that manages the available resources of a computer and 'controls' the applications (or programs) that run on it.

In Europe, Vista is available in four main editions. **Home Basic**, the cheapest, is suitable for existing PCs, but we would not recommend it. The **Home Premium** edition has many extra features, such as Windows Media Centre, the Aero Desktop experience and 3D graphics. The **Business** edition substitutes business networking and hardware protection for the Media Centre facility, and the **Ultimate** edition which, as its name suggests, includes everything, is really for larger businesses.

Most home PCs come with the Home Premium edition pre-loaded and users will almost certainly find that this contains all the facilities they will need. We have used this edition to write this book. There has been a lot of negative media coverage about Vista as an operating system, but we have it on several of our PCs and, apart from one scanner not being supported, have had no problems at all. It seems that a lot of prejudice could be involved!

The Vista Desktop

By default, when you switch on your PC and enter your user details, Vista opens the Welcome Center in the middle of the Desktop, the working area of your computer screen, as shown in Fig. 1.1 on the next page.

Fig. 1.1 Our Vista Opening Screen

What appears in the Welcome Center window can depend on the make of your computer. As shown above, in the top third are details of the currently logged user with particulars of the PC's software and hardware.

In the middle of the window, under the **Get started with Windows** heading, are six icons you can left-click with your mouse to get easy access to some programs and features such as the **View computer details** and **Connect to the Internet**. Clicking the **Show all 14 items** link below these, opens even more for you to explore. Perhaps **What's new in Windows Vista**, would be a good place to start.

What you are offered in the bottom third of the Welcome Center window depends on what your PC supplier has put there.

If you don't want to see the Welcome Center window every time you start Vista, just left-click the check box at the bottom left of the window to remove the tick. You can always get it back from the **System and Maintenance** section of the **Control Panel** – more about this later.

The Vista Sidebar

On the right of the Vista Desktop is the **Sidebar** shown here, which can hold mini-programs known as 'gadgets'. These show real time information or provide easy access to frequently used tools, such as the **Clock**, **Calendar**, **Weather** and **Currency** gadgets in our example.

To add gadgets to the **Sidebar**, click the **Gadgets** icon  at the top of the bar and choose from the options in the window that opens. You can also **Get more gadgets online** from there.

Fig. 1.2 Changing the Clock Gadget Settings

To close a gadget, click the red **Close** icon ⊠ which appears when you move the pointer over it. With some gadgets you can also click a blue **Tool** icon and change its settings in a window, like that in Fig. 1.2. For the clock you can choose between 8 different styles and set whatever time you want, but these days we usually find our computer time is correct.

The Sidebar and its gadgets can be very useful, but they do take up space on your Desktop, and your PC takes longer to start up when they are active. If this becomes a problem, you can close the Sidebar by right-clicking it and selecting the **Close Sidebar** option. To open it again, right-click the **Windows Sidebar** icon in the Notification Area of the Taskbar, (see next section) and click **Open** in the context menu shown in Fig. 1.3.

Fig. 1.3

The Taskbar

The **Taskbar** is located at the bottom of the Vista Desktop, but you can 'drag' it to any border of the screen. This is the area of the Desktop that contains the **Start** button 🔵 and **Quick Launch** bar on the left, the **Notification Area** on the right, and buttons for all your open programs in the middle.

Fig. 1.4 The Vista Taskbar

When you open a program, or a window, a button for it is placed on the Taskbar to the right of the **Quick Launch** buttons. In Fig. 1.4 we show **Word Pro** our word processor, the **Welcome Center** and the **Control Panel** open. With Vista you can preview the contents of an item on the Taskbar by hovering the mouse pointer over its button. A thumbnail appears showing a miniature version of the window. This works even if the window has a video or animation playing. In Fig. 1.5 below, we show the preview of what was open in our word processor at the time.

Fig. 1.5 Previewing an Item on the Taskbar

Left-clicking an open application button on the Taskbar makes that application active, opens it on the Desktop and displays its button on the Taskbar in a darker shade of grey (the **Welcome Center** in Fig. 1.4 above). So now, using the Taskbar, you can always see what applications you have open, which is the active one, what it contains, and quickly switch between them. Very neat.

The Start Button and Menu

Vista should start up as soon as you switch on your PC, so you don't have to start it manually. Then, clicking the **Start** button 🔵 on the left end of the Taskbar, or pressing the Windows key 🔳, opens the **Start** menu which gives you access to all the applications and settings on your computer. Fig. 1.6 shows a typical Start menu, as well as the Recycle Bin icon.

Fig. 1.6 The Vista Start Menu

The menu in the left pane has two parts. You can add shortcuts to your most frequently used programs in the top section. Below the line, Vista automatically puts shortcuts to the applications you have used most recently. So this section can change as you use your PC. Your shortcut lists will of course be totally different from ours in Fig. 1.6 above.

In the black pane on the right are shortcuts to Documents, Pictures, Music, Games, Computer, Control Panel, etc., which are normally common to all users.

Just one left-click with your mouse on any of the shortcuts on the Start Menu will open the application or process.

The Quick Launch Bar

 You can just click any of the three buttons, or icons, on the **Quick Launch** bar (located to the right of the **Start** button 🔵) to open, or launch, that application. From left to right the default icons are: **Show desktop** 🖳, **Switch between windows** 🖼, and **Internet Explorer** 🅴.

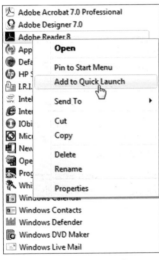

Fig. 1.7 Adding to the Quick Launch Bar

You can easily add icons to, or remove them from, the **Quick Launch** bar to reflect the way you work.

To add an icon, click the **Start** button 🔵, then **All Programs**, find the program in the **Start** menu listing, right-click it, and select the **Add to Quick Launch** option, pointed to here in Fig. 1.7. The program icon should then appear in the **Quick Launch** bar as in Fig. 1.8 below.

If this option is not available to you in the context menu, you can also drag the program's icon to the **Quick Launch** bar.

To remove an icon from the **Quick Launch** bar, right-click it and select **Delete**, followed by **Yes**. It is well worth spending a few minutes adding your most used programs to this bar, you will save yourself a lot of time.

If at any time you see double chevrons ⟩⟩ instead of your icons, you can re-size the **Quick Launch** bar. First, unlock the Taskbar by right-clicking an empty area on it and clearing the check mark against the **Lock the Taskbar** option. Then drag the 'toolbar sizing' handle ▌ to the right until you have room for all of your icons. You can then lock the Taskbar again.

Fig. 1.8 Re-sizing the Bar

The Notification Area

 This is the area, also called the **System Tray**, on the right of the Taskbar that includes a digital clock and icons showing the status of specific programs and settings. The icons you see depend on your computer and how it is set up.

When you move the pointer over an icon, an information bubble opens showing the name or the status for that setting. Pointing to the **Network** icon, for instance, displays information about whether you are connected to a network, as shown in Fig. 1.9.

Fig. 1.9 Network Icon

Double-clicking an icon opens its program or setting. Try double-clicking the **Volume** icon to open the volume controls so you can control the volume of the speakers attached to your PC, or built into your laptop.

This part of the Taskbar is called the Notification Area

Fig. 1.10 Notification Message

because the icons display a small pop-up window, or notification, when something has happened on your system. In Fig. 1.10, for example, a virus scan had just started.

Vista hides icons when you don't use them for a while, but you can click the **Show hidden icons** icon to temporarily show them again.

Windows Aero

Microsoft call 'Windows Aero' the "premium visual experience of Vista". If your PC is capable of 3D graphics and you have at least Vista Home Premium you should be able to see new window colours and transparent borders, and get the **Flip 3D** feature, shown in Fig. 1.11, when you click the **Switch between windows** button on the **Quick Launch** toolbar.

Fig. 1.11 Aero's Flip 3D in Action

Try using the scroll wheel on your mouse and see the windows on the screen change position in really spectacular fashion. To open a particular window, point to it and left-click.

Another way to quickly identify the window you want when you have several open is to use the so-called **Flip** feature. This lets you flip through open windows by using the **Alt+Tab** keyboard combination (keep the **Alt** key depressed and press the **Tab** key). What you see on the screen should be something like we show in Fig. 1.12 below.

Fig. 1.12 Window's Flip Feature

It is very easy to control Aero and Vista's other visual features by right-clicking on an empty part of the Desktop and selecting the **Personalize** option ✿ Personalize from the context menu. This opens the window shown in Fig. 1.13 on the next page, in which you can customise most of Vista's features. You can spend many happy hours here!

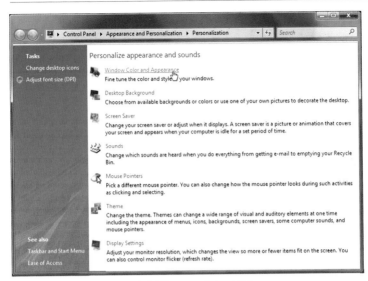

Fig. 1.13 Personalising Vista

Clicking the **Window Color and Appearance** heading, pointed to above, opens the very colourful window shown below for you to play with.

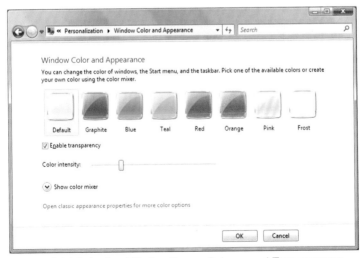

Fig. 1.14 Selecting Window Frame Colours and Transparency

User Accounts

Vista makes it possible for several people to share a computer (a family maybe) with each having their own set-up. This is done using individual User Accounts. Each account tells Vista what files and folders the holder can access, what changes he or she can make to the computer, and controls personal preferences, such as Desktop backgrounds and colour schemes.

 At the top of the **Start** menu the name of the current user is displayed with a picture or icon above it, as shown here and earlier in Fig. 1.6. Left-clicking this icon opens the User Accounts window shown below in Fig. 1.15.

Fig. 1.15 The Vista User Accounts Window

This is where the person logged on can create or change their user password, choose a different icon, change the name or type of their account, etc.

When you log on to Vista, the Welcome screen displays the accounts that are available on the computer. You can make life easier, as we do, by only using one account, but then everyone that uses the PC has the same access to everything. If that isn't a problem this is by far the easiest way to go.

Running Programs

As an operating system, Vista manages the other programs you run on your PC, such as word processors, spreadsheets, databases and games. You can double-click a shortcut icon on your Desktop to open a program, but the **Start** menu (Fig. 1.6) is the main way to access your computer's programs, folders, and settings. As we saw on page 5, clicking the **Start** button on the left end of the Taskbar, opens the **Start** menu. To open a program shown in the left pane of this menu, just click it. The program opens and the **Start** menu closes.

If the program you want isn't listed but you know its name, just start typing the name into the **Search** box at the bottom of the left pane.

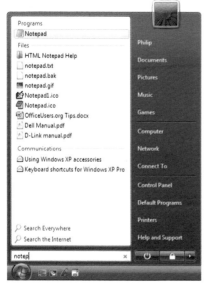

Fig. 1.16 Searching for Notepad

In Fig. 1.16, we wanted to open the Notepad text editor, so we started typing its name in the **Search** box. The left pane instantly displayed search results, right from the first letter typed, and the list became more selective as each new letter was added.

What we were looking for soon appeared at the top of the list under the **Programs** heading, as shown here. Clicking it opened the Notepad program and closed the **Start** menu.

This method saves you having to find the program in a menu, and you don't even need to click in the **Search** box before you start typing.

If all else fails, click **All Programs** above the **Search** box and the left pane will show a long list of programs in alphabetical order, followed by a list of folders, as shown here in Fig. 1.17.

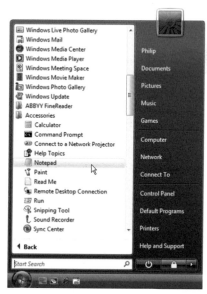

Fig. 1.17 The All Programs List with the Accessories Folder Opened

This shows some of the contents of the **All Programs** list on one of our computers, and the contents of the Windows **Accessories** folder.

Note that in Vista, programs are given distinctive icons in these lists. Clicking on the Notepad option, starts the program in its own window.

Folders, like the **Accessories** folder, have a different icon and can contain other folders, documents, programs or other items. If you don't know what a program does, move the pointer over its icon or name. A message box should appear with a description of the program.

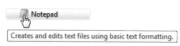

To close an opened folder on this list, left-click it again. To get back to the programs you saw when you first opened the **Start** menu, click **Back** at the bottom of the menu (Fig. 1.17).

New to Windows Vista is another kind of folder, called a **Virtual Folder** which is simply a saved search. Whenever you open a saved search, it will search your computer again to find all the files that match what you are looking for (see page 31 for more on this).

Changing the Start Menu

As mentioned earlier, Vista has the ability to adapt the first of its two-column menus to the way you use your PC. It keeps track of what features and programs you use the most and adds them to the list at the bottom of the left column. For example, if you use **WordPad** a couple of times by selecting it from the **Accessories** sub-menu, next time you click the **Start** button you will see this application pinned to the bottom half of the **Start** menu. This saves time as you don't have to scroll through menu lists to find the application you want to use.

Fig. 1.18 Using the Context Menu

To remove an application from the left pane of the **Start** menu, right-click it with your mouse and select the option **Remove from this list**, as shown in Fig. 1.18. This removes the name of the application from the list, but not the application itself from your hard disc.

You also have a menu option to **Pin to Start Menu** any selected program. This adds the program to the top half of the left pane of the **Start** menu which is a more permanent list.

When some programs are installed on your PC they place a shortcut icon on your Desktop, like that shown here. Right-clicking this displays similar options to those above, so you can pin the program to either the **Start** menu or the **Quick Launch** bar.

Ending a PC Session

Fig. 1.19 Vista's
Shut Down Options

When you have finished for the day, it is important to save your work and 'turn off' your computer properly, both to save energy and to protect your data. With Vista there are several options for ending the session, all available from the Power buttons at the bottom of the **Start** menu as shown in Fig. 1.19. Clicking the **Start** button 🔵 and hovering the pointer over the right arrow button ▶, will open the options menu shown.

From here you can select to **Switch User**, **Log Off** the current user and leave the computer running so another user can log on, **Lock** the Computer so that it needs a password before you can carry on working, **Restart** the computer to clear the memory settings and reset Windows, put the PC in **Sleep** mode in which your work is saved and the computer put in low-power mode, use **Hibernate**, an even deeper sleep, where your work is saved to disc and when you restart everything is as you left it, or **Shut Down** the computer completely.

The **Lock this computer** button 🔒 also locks your PC so that you need a password to access it, and, by default, the **Power** button ⏻ puts your PC to sleep. To wake it again press the power button on the computer case.

If there are updates to install on your computer, the **Power** button changes to 🔘. When you click it in this form, Vista installs the updates and then shuts down the PC.

Mobile PC users just have to close the lid!

Sleep and Hibernation modes often don't seem to work correctly. If this happens on your PC we suggest you go to the Web site **www.vistax64.com/tutorials**, click the **Power Management** icon and open the **Power Options and Sleep Mode Problems** tutorial. Good luck, but we have solved all our Power problems here.

2

The Vista Environment

In Vista every user starts with a set of data folders called simply **Documents**, **Pictures**, **Music**, etc. To see your folders in a Vista Explorer window, click the **Start** button ⏺ and then click your log-on name at the top of the **Start** menu (see Fig. 1.6). This opens a window similar to Fig. 2.1 below.

Fig. 2.1 A Set of Personal Folders

Don't expect the contents of yours to look much like ours above, as we have added extra folders! The left pane of the Explorer window, called the **Navigation** pane, lists your **Favorite Links** and gives you access to a tree view by clicking the **Folders** button Folders ⌃ at the bottom. The right pane lists the folders and files in the selected location.

Clicking a link in the **Navigation** pane opens the contents of that folder in the right pane. Double-clicking a folder in the right pane will open it and display its contents.

Clicking , (the **Folders** button), at the bottom of the **Navigation** pane opens a tree view display of the folders associated with the window, similar to that in Fig. 2.2.

The **Folders** tree gives you instant navigation starting from your Desktop. It could not be simpler – no more hunting deep through endless 'Documents and Settings' to find what you want!

To close the **Folders** tree, left-click the Folders button, which now has a down arrow.

Fig. 2.2 The Folders Tree View

Parts of a Window

On the next page we show a typical Vista Explorer window with its constituent parts labelled and later described. We use the word 'Windows' to refer to the whole Vista Windows environment, and 'windows' to refer to document or setting windows.

You may have noticed by now that the buttons on the toolbars of the different Vista windows change automatically to reflect the type of work you can do in that type of window.

Pictures and **Videos** windows, for example, have a **Slide Show** button ▣ Slide Show , whereas **Music** windows have **Play** ▶ Play and **Play All** ▶ Play all buttons.

By default in Vista, menus are not shown. To see the **Menu** bar in a Vista window press the **Alt** key, or click the **Organize** button and select the **Layout, Menu Bar** option.

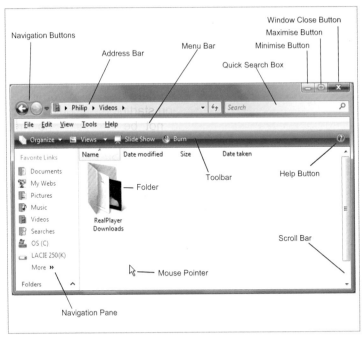

Fig. 2.3 Components of a Vista Explorer Window

The typical Explorer window is subdivided into several areas which have the following functions:

Area	Function
Minimise button	Left-clicking the **Minimise** button stores a window and its contents as an icon on the **Taskbar**. Clicking on such an icon will restore the window.
Maximise button	Left-clicking the **Maximise** button fills the screen with the active window. When that happens, the **Maximise** button changes to a **Restore Down** button which can be used to restore the window to its former size.

Close button	The extreme top right button that you click to close a window.
Navigation buttons	The **Go Back** (left) button takes you to the previous display, while the **Go Forward** (right) button takes you to the next display. The down-arrow ▼ gives access to **Recent Pages**.
Address bar 	Shows the location of the current folder. You can change locations here, or switch to an Internet Explorer window by typing a Web address (URL).
Quick search box	The box in which you type your search criteria. As you start typing the first few letters, the displayed files filter down to just the matching terms. This makes finding your files much easier.
Menu bar	The bar which only displays if you press the **Alt** key. It allows you to choose from several menu options. Clicking on a menu item displays the pull-down menu associated with it.
Toolbar	A bar of icons that you click to carry out some common actions. The icons displayed on the toolbar depend on the type of window.
Scroll bars/buttons	The bars/buttons at the extreme right and bottom of each window (or pane within a window) that contain a scroll box/button. Clicking on these allows you to see parts of a document that might not be visible in that size window.
Mouse pointer	The arrow which appears when the pointer is placed over menus, scroll bars, buttons, and folder lists.

With Vista's Explorer windows you can activate three additional panes by clicking the **Organize** toolbar button, selecting **Layout** from the drop-down menu, and clicking one of the options which have the following functions:

Option	*Function*
Search pane	To limit areas of search.
Details pane	To display information on an item.
Preview pane	To preview the contents of a selected file without opening it.
Navigation pane	Shows links and folders so that you can easily navigate around your PC.

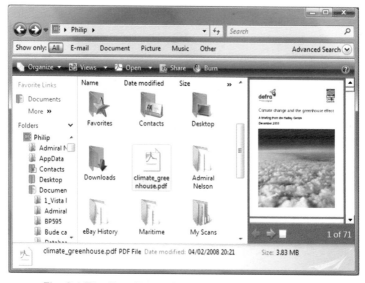

Fig. 2.4 The Four Panes Surrounding the Display Area

Fig. 2.4 above shows a window with all these panes open. The **Search** pane is located above the toolbar, the **Navigation** pane on the left, the **Preview** pane on the right, and the **Details** pane at the bottom of the screen.

Menu Bar Options

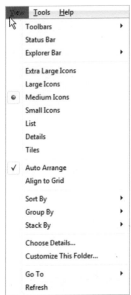

Each window's menu bar option (you can display it by pressing the **Alt** key) has associated with it a pull-down sub-menu. To activate a menu option, highlight it and click the left mouse button. To action a sub-menu option, highlight it and left-click the mouse.

A typical **View** sub-menu is shown here in Fig. 2.5.

Items on the sub-menu marked with an arrow to their right ▶, open up additional options when selected.

Most Vista system applications offer the **File**, **Edit**, **View**, **Tools** and **Help** menu options.

Fig. 2.5 A Typical Vista Sub-menu

Note: Having activated a menu, whether from the menu bar or a right-click, you can close it without taking any further action by simply left-clicking the mouse pointer somewhere else on the screen, or by simply pressing the **Esc** key.

Dialogue Boxes

Three periods after a sub-menu option or command, means that a dialogue box will open when the option or command is selected. A dialogue box is used for the insertion of additional information.

To see a dialogue box, click the **Start** button and select the **Computer** menu option. Next, press the **Alt** key to display the **Menu bar**, click **Tools** and on the drop-down sub-menu select **Folder Options**. This opens the Folder Options dialogue box with its General tab selected. In Fig. 2.6 on the next page we show this dialogue box with its View tab selected so that you can see different types of option lists.

Fig. 2.6 The Folder Options Dialogue Box

When a dialogue box opens, you can use the **Tab** key to move the dotted rectangle, or focus, from one field to another, or more easily, you can use the mouse.

Some dialogue boxes contain List boxes which show a column of available choices. If there are more choices than can be seen in the area provided, use the scroll bars to reveal them, as above.

Dialogue boxes may contain Check boxes ☑, which offer a list of features you can switch on or off. Selected options show a tick in the box against the option name.

Another feature available is the Option, or Radio, button ◉, with a list of mutually exclusive items. The default choice is marked with a blue dot. Unavailable options are dimmed.

To cancel a dialogue box, either press the **Cancel** button, or the **Esc** key enough times to close the dialogue box and then the menu system.

Taskbar and Start Menu Properties

As we saw in the last chapter, at the bottom of the Desktop screen to the right of the **Start** button 🔵 is the **Taskbar**. This is used to quickly start programs (from the **Quick Launch** bar), or to switch between them.

To display the **Taskbar** properties, right-click an empty part of it and select **Properties** from the context menu.

This tabbed box lets you configure the **Taskbar** by locking it, auto-hiding it, or keeping it on top of any other windows. From here you can also control whether the **Quick Launch** bar is shown.

You might have noticed by now that as more buttons are placed on the **Taskbar** their size shrinks slightly, but only up to a point. After that point, common entries are grouped together

Fig. 2.7 The Taskbar and Start Menu Properties Dialogue Box

provided the **Group similar taskbar buttons** box is ticked, as in Fig. 2.7. To see details relating to a grouped button, move the mouse pointer over it on the **Taskbar** to get a display like in Fig. 2.8a, or left-click it to open a list of components, as in Fig. 2.8b, both on the next page. To close a group of running programs, right-click their **Taskbar** button and select **Close Group**.

Do investigate the other tab screens of the **Taskbar and Start Menu Properties** dialogue box (Fig. 2.7), to see how you can configure your PC to work and look best for you.

(a)   (b)

Fig. 2.8 Grouped Taskbar Entries

Changing the Date and Time

Fig. 2.9 Date and Time
Properties Dialogue Box

On the far right of the **Taskbar** is a digital clock showing the current time as given by the internal clock of your PC. Left-clicking the time display, opens the pop-up window shown in Fig. 2.9. Clicking the **Change date and time settings** link on this opens the **Date and Time** box, so that you can control your clock.

Fig. 2.10 The Date and Time Box

As you can see here, the clock changes automatically between Summer and Winter times. You can set it to show extra clocks for different time zones.

On the Internet Time tab you can even set your clock to synchronise with an Internet time server, so it should always be correct.

Manipulating Windows

To use any Vista program effectively, you need to be able to work with a series of windows, and make a window active, move it, or re-size it so that you can see all of it.

Changing the active window – If you have several windows open on the screen, you can make one active by simply clicking it with the left mouse button, or, if it is not visible, click its icon on the **Taskbar**.

Moving a window – To move a window (or a dialogue box), point to its title bar with the mouse, as shown in Fig. 2.11, and drag it with the left button depressed until it is where you want on the screen, then release the mouse button. You can only do this if the window does not occupy the full screen and it has a maximise button  visible.

Fig. 2.11 Moving a Window

Minimising and maximising windows – To minimise a window into a **Taskbar** icon, maybe to free up Desktop space, left-click the **Minimize** button ▭ in the upper-right corner of the window.

To maximise a window so that it fills the entire screen, left-click the **Maximize** button ▭.

A window that has been minimised or maximised can be returned to its original size and position on the screen by either clicking on its **Taskbar** icon to expand it to a window, or clicking on the **Restore Down** button  of a maximised window, to reduce it to its former size.

Re-sizing a window – You can change the size of a window with the mouse by first moving the window so that the side you want to change is visible, then placing the mouse pointer on the edge of the window, or on a corner, so that it changes to a two-headed arrow, then dragging this arrow to get the size you want.

Closing a window – Any window can be closed at any time, to save screen space and memory, by left-clicking its Close button .

Help with Vista

Whatever you are doing in Vista, help is not very far away. Just click the **Start** button , then click the **Help and Support** menu option to open the main Help window, shown in Fig. 2.12 below.

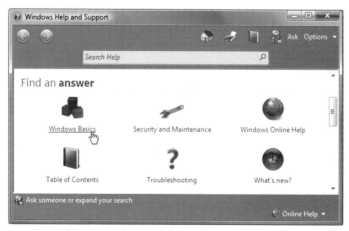

Fig. 2.12 Windows Vista Help and Support

You can click one of the options in the **Find an answer** section, or use the **Browse Help** button to open a browsable list as shown in Fig. 2.13.

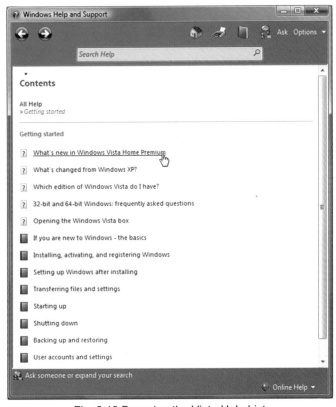

Fig. 2.13 Browsing the Vista Help List

The **Search Help** box gives you access to a very powerful Help search facility. Type the word or phrase you want help with into the text box and click the **Search Help** button . Try it, it's the method we have used most over the months.

When you are in a Vista Explorer window, you can also click the **Get Help** button on the toolbar, to get specific help on the type of window you are working with.

3

Files, Folders and Photos

On a computer, a **file** contains related information, such as a word-processed letter, a spreadsheet, a digital photo, a video, or a music track. Vista represents files with icons in its Explorer windows, as shown in Fig. 3.1, so you can tell what kind of file an icon represents just by looking at it.

| Text File | Photo | Word File | Excel File | Video |

Fig. 3.1 File Icons in a Documents Window

You control the size of the icons in the window's **View** sub-menu (page 28). Fig. 3.1 above, has **Large Icons**.

A **folder** is just a container in which you can store files or other folders. Arranging files into logical groups in folders makes it easier to locate and work with them.

Fig. 3.2 Folders in a Vista Documents Window

By default, Vista provides four special folders for each user, called **Documents**, **Pictures**, **Music**, and **Games**, all of which can be accessed from the **Start** menu. In each of these folders you can place files and other folders.

We recommend that you carry on with this structure, so that photos and folders created for photos should go in the **Pictures** folder, word processor and spreadsheet files and folders would go in the **Documents** folder, etc.

In this way, when you click the **Start** button ●, the folders will be available for you on the top-right of the **Start** menu, as shown here.

You can change how your file and folder icons appear in Vista's Explorer windows with the **Views** 'slider' menu on the toolbar of every folder, shown open in Fig. 3.3 below.

Open the folder you want to change. Click the down-arrow next to **Views** on the toolbar and move the slider up or down to change the appearance of the icons.

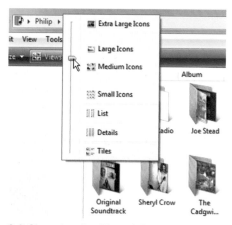

Fig. 3.3 Changing the Size of File and Folder Icons

As shown, the slider has seven rest positions between **Tiles** and **Extra Large Icons**. You can fine-tune the size of the icons by moving the slider to any point between these positions. As you do this, keep your eye on the **Views** button itself. It changes to show the currently selected view. Little touches like this make Vista a pleasure to use.

Creating a New Folder

To create a new folder, open the Vista folder you want it to be in, by left-clicking the **Start** button ● and clicking it in the **Start** menu, as we did for the **Pictures** folder in Fig. 3.4 below (in your case the contents will obviously be different).

Fig. 3.4 Creating a New Folder

Next, left-click the **Organize** toolbar button , and select the **New Folder** option, as shown in Fig. 3.4.

When Vista creates a new folder it gives it the original name **New Folder**, places it alphabetically in the list of existing items, and highlights the name ready for you to rename it, as shown here. You just type a new name, say, **Photos**, over the default name.

Perhaps an easier way to create a new folder is to go to the location, or folder, where you want to create it, right-click a blank area in the window, select **New**, **Folder** from the context menu, type a name for the new folder, and press **Enter**. This is the way we usually use.

There are several ways to rename a file or folder at any time, but the easiest is probably to select the folder or file you want to rename, then left-click in the name area to select the old name and just type the new name.

Searching for Files and Folders

Vista has a new **Instant Search** facility which appears on the **Start** menu, immediately above the **Start** button ⊕, and in every Explorer type window. These can help you locate files, e-mail messages, and other items on your PC. Just type a file name, a property, or some of the text in a file, and **Search** should quickly find it for you.

To find a specific file or folder located anywhere on your PC, open the **Start** menu and start typing in the **Instant Search** box. As you type, the left pane instantly displays search results, right from the first letter typed, with the list becoming more selective as each new letter is added. Vista groups the results in categories as shown in our example in Fig. 3.5.

Fig. 3.5 Searching for Files

If the file or folder you want is listed, simply click it to open it.

If not, you can click the **Search Everywhere** link at the bottom of the list, to open the search in a Search Folder as shown in Fig. 3.6.

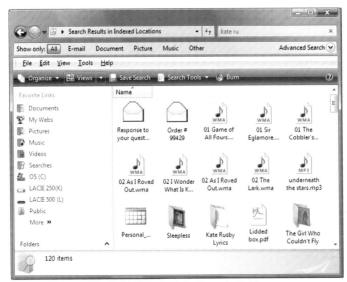

Fig. 3.6 Results in a Search Folder

In a Search Folder the default search is for **All** types of files, but you can narrow down the search criteria, by selecting to display only **E-mail** messages, or **Document**, **Picture** or **Music** files.

With Vista you can use the **Save Search** button on the toolbar to save the search criteria you have used together with the search results in a **Virtual** folder. Opening this folder in the future, will start a new search of the same type.

If you know what folder a file is in, you can open it and use the **Quick Search** box in the folder window to carry out your search in the same way.

Vista's search facility is very powerful but it can be somewhat confusing, to say the least. If you need more help coming to terms with it, we suggest you look in the Help system (have another look at page 25 if necessary).

A search for **Tips for finding files** is a very good place to start. If you still need more help, you could then try the links at the bottom of the page.

Working with Files and Folders

The longer you work with a computer the more files and folders you accumulate. To keep things manageable you need at least to be able to copy, move and delete them.

Selecting Files and Folders – In Windows you have to select an item before you can do something with it. When it is selected in Vista, a file or folder is given a pale blue surround, as shown in Fig. 3.7 below.

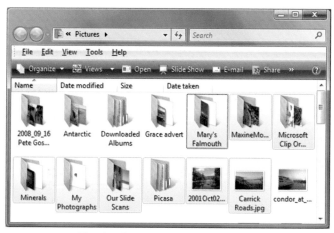

Fig. 3.7 Selected Files and Folders

To select one file or folder in a window just click it. To select several objects you have three main options:

- If they form a contiguous list, as in Fig. 3.7 above, left-click the first in the list, then with the **Shift** key depressed, click the last in the list.

- To select random objects, hold the **Ctrl** key down and left-click them, one by one.

- To select all the items in a window just use the **Ctrl+A** keyboard shortcut.

To cancel a selection, click in an empty area of the window.

Copying Files and Folders – When you *copy* a file or folder to somewhere else, the original version of the folder or file is not altered or removed, but when you *move* a folder or file to a new location, the original is actually deleted.

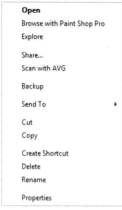

Open
Browse with Paint Shop Pro
Explore

Share...
Scan with AVG

Backup

Send To   ▸

Cut
Copy

Create Shortcut
Delete
Rename

Properties

Fig. 3.8 The File
Context Menu

To copy selected items into another folder, right-click them and choose the **Copy** option from the shortcut menu as shown in Fig. 3.8.

The selected files are then copied to the Windows **Clipboard** which is a temporary storage area in memory where text, graphics and files are stored with the Windows **Cut** and **Copy** commands.

All you need to do now is navigate to the destination folder, right-click in it and select the **Paste** option from the context, or shortcut, menu that opens.

Moving Files and Folders – To move selected items into a target folder, choose the **Cut** option from the shortcut menu (Fig. 3.8). This removes them from their current place and copies them to the Windows **Clipboard** so that you can **Paste** them into the target folder.

Using Drag and Drop – If you are happy using the mouse, you can drag selected objects in one folder or between two open folders, with the **Ctrl** key depressed, to copy them.

If you don't use the **Ctrl** key you will move them. You need to be careful with this method though, as it is easy to drop your precious files and folders in the wrong location. You then have to spend 'hours' looking for them!

Creating Desktop Shortcuts – With Vista you can put a shortcut to any program file or document on your Desktop or in a folder. Shortcuts are quick ways to get to the items you use often; they save you having to dig into menus to access them.

One program that you might want to access quickly, to say write a quick letter, is Vista's **WordPad**, so we will step you through the process of placing a shortcut to it on the Desktop.

WordPad is in the **Accessories** folder, so to locate it use the **Start**, **All Programs**, **Accessories** menu option. Next, highlight **WordPad**, right-click it, and select the **Send To**, **Desktop (create shortcut)** option, as shown in Fig. 3.9.

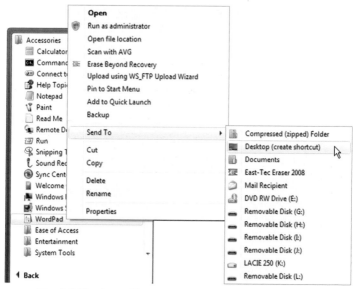

Fig. 3.9 Placing a Shortcut to WordPad on the Desktop

As is usual with Vista there is another way to create a shortcut on the Desktop that we usually use. First find the program in the **Start**, **All Programs** list and drag it to the Desktop with the right mouse button depressed. When the mouse button is released, select the **Create Shortcuts Here** option from the menu that opens. This places the new shortcut on the Desktop and you can drag it to the location on your screen that you want. Fig. 3.10 on the facing page, shows the sequence graphically.

Double-clicking a shortcut icon on the Desktop is much easier than digging deep into the menus to open a program.

Fig. 3.10 Placing a Shortcut by Dragging to the Desktop

Deleting Files or Folders – To delete or remove files or folders, first select them in an Explorer window, and then either select the **Organize**, **Delete** ✗ Delete   option, right-click them and select **Delete**, or press the **Del** key on the keyboard. All of these methods open a message box giving you the chance to abort the operation by selecting **No**.

Deleting a single folder or file displays the dialogue box shown in Fig 3.11.

Fig. 3.11 The Delete Folder Warning Box

In any of these cases, to carry on with the deletion select the **Yes** option.

Now is the time to do some housekeeping and delete any duplicate or unwanted image files. Take care though and make sure you really don't want them! Do carry out this suggestion as we need to demonstrate what happens to deleted items next.

The Recycle Bin

As you can see from the **Delete Folder** message box on the previous page, by default all files or folders deleted from a hard disc, are actually placed in a holding folder named the **Recycle Bin**.

If you open the **Recycle Bin**, by double-clicking its Desktop icon, shown here and earlier in Fig. 1.5, you will see that it is just a special folder. It lists all the files, folders, icons and shortcuts that have been deleted from fixed drives since it was last emptied, as shown in Fig. 3.12 below. To see the display as it appears below, use the **Views**, **Medium Icons** menu option.

Fig. 3.12 The Recycle Bin Folder Showing Deleted Items

Vista keeps a record of the original locations of the deleted files and folders, so that it can restore them if necessary. To restore all the items in the **Recycle Bin**, click the **Restore all items** button. To finally delete its contents click the **Empty the Recycle Bin** option. Beware though, you won't be able to get the data back again.

To restore specific files or folders, first select them, then click the **Restore** button. To delete an item, select it and press the **Delete** keyboard key.

Every now and then you should open the **Recycle Bin** and delete unwanted files or folders to free up hard disc space.

Sorting and Filtering

By clicking the headings above the file list in a Vista Explorer folder, you can control what files are displayed in the window (filtering) and in what order (sorting).

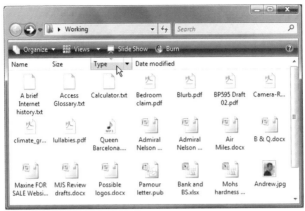

Fig. 3.13 A Folder Sorted by File Type

Just clicking a header will sort the displayed files based on the header. The **Name** header sorts alphabetically, **Size** sorts by file size, etc. Clicking the header again reverses the sort order. In Fig. 3.13 we sorted the files into their types by clicking the **Type** header, as shown.

You filter your files when you only want files with a particular property to be displayed. You do this by clicking the arrow to the right of the heading that you want to filter by. The drop-down menu that opens, depends on the heading clicked. In Fig. 3.14 for instance, on the next page, you can select to only show files of specific types, by ticking the boxes next to the types you want.

You can also **Stack** the displayed files, where all of the files in the view are arranged into piles, or stacks. To see the files that are contained in an individual stack, just double-click it. A **Group**, on the other hand, displays a sequential list of all of the grouped files. You will need to play with these options to get to know how they work.

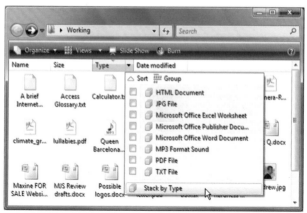

Fig. 3.14 Filtering a Folder by File Type

Copying to a CD or DVD

To copy files or folders to a CD or DVD, you will need a recorder fitted to your PC and a supply of suitable discs.

By default, Vista uses the new **Live File System** format for burning CDs and DVDs. With this format you can copy selected files immediately and as often as you want straight to the disc in the recorder drive, just like a USB flash drive or floppy disc. BUT, the discs produced are only compatible with Windows XP and later versions of Windows. For more information on this, we suggest you search the Vista help system for **Which CD or DVD format should I use?**

To start the process, locate and select the files or folders you want to copy to disc. Make sure that the selected files or folders do not exceed 650 MB for a standard CD or 4.7 GB for a standard DVD. Click the **Burn** button on the Explorer window toolbar, as shown in Fig. 3.15.

Insert a blank recordable or rewritable CD or DVD in the recorder when asked, and type a title in the **Burn a Disc** box that opens (Fig. 3.16).

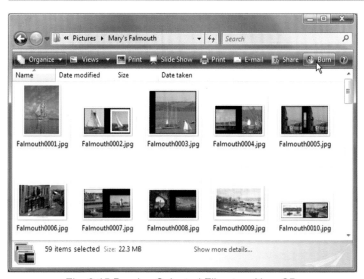

Fig. 3.15 Burning Selected Files to a New CD

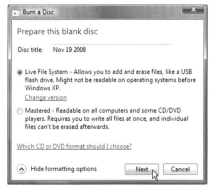

Fig. 3.16 Preparing a Blank Disc

With a new disc, when you click the **Next** button, Vista will format the disc after first checking with you. This took some 15 minutes for us with a new CD-RW disc. A DVD would take longer. But it only needs doing once.

The burning process is then started and the selected files are copied to the disc very quickly. You can leave the disc in the drive while you are working and copy more files to it, or delete files from it, whenever you want. This method is excellent for making manual backup type copies of your data.

Photographs

As we have seen, the **Pictures** folder is provided by Vista for storing all of your digital pictures. It is the default location for importing pictures from your digital camera or scanner. We put most of our images in sub-folders of the **Pictures** folder, as it makes it easier to keep track of them. The folder below holds some splendid photos from the US Antarctic Program Web Portal of the National Science Foundation.

Fig. 3.17 A Folder of Photos

You may have noticed by now that the toolbar buttons change depending on what you are doing. Fig. 3.17 shows a typical **Pictures** folder toolbar with no files selected. As soon as you select a file, 4 extra buttons are placed on the bar, as shown below.

Fig. 3.18 An Extended Pictures Folder Toolbar

We have already used the **Organize**, **Views** and **Burn** buttons, so perhaps it's time we had a look at the other toolbar options.

Previewing Photos

If you double-click a photo, or click the **Preview** toolbar button , it is opened by default in the Windows Photo Gallery described on the next page. Clicking the down-arrow next to the **Preview** button gives you a list of programs which you can use to edit the selected picture, as shown in Fig. 3.19. For you, this list might be different, depending on the programs you have installed on your PC.

Fig. 3.19 Photo Editors

Printing Photos

Selecting pictures and clicking the **Print** button , displays the **Print Pictures** window shown below.

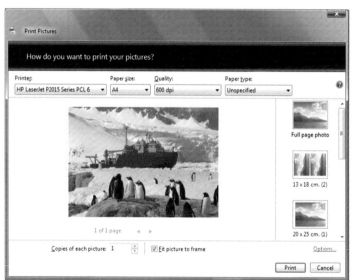

Fig. 3.20 Printing Photos from a Vista Window

From here you can select the **Printer** to be used, **Paper size**, **Quality** of print, **Paper Type** and a variety of layouts for your pictures. All you have to do then is click the **Print** button.

The Windows Photo Gallery

Double-clicking a picture in an Explorer folder, or clicking the **Preview** toolbar button [🖼 Preview], opens the **Windows Photo Gallery** preview window, as shown in Fig. 3.21.

Fig. 3.21 A Windows Photo Gallery Preview

The **Fix** button on the toolbar opens tools for you to perform simple photo fixes, such as adjusting the exposure and colour balance, cropping a picture so only part of it is displayed, and removing red-eye.

You can use the buttons at the bottom of the screen to navigate through the current folder, view the pictures in your folder as a slide show, zoom in or out, rotate the image, and delete it from your hard disc.

To organise your photos, click the **Go To Gallery** button on the toolbar to open the full Photo Gallery shown in Fig. 3.22. You can also open this Vista program with the **Start**, **All Programs**, **Windows Photo Gallery** menu command. This is where you can sort your photos and display them in different ways: by date, using star ratings, or using descriptive tags.

Fig. 3.22 The Photo Gallery Window

Once your photos have been fixed and organised, you can save a folder of photos to a blank CD or DVD, or click the **Make a Movie** button to make a slide show using Windows Movie Maker. The **Help** button may be of use here!

Slide Shows

To see your photos as a continuous slide show, click the centre button of the navigation bar at the bottom of the Photo Gallery screen shown here and above, or press the **F11** key.

Fig. 3.23 Starting a Slide Show

The slide show will play all of the pictures in the current view of Photo Gallery, or any photos that you have selected, but you may need to be patient, as it seems to take a few minutes to start the first time it is used in a session.

If you move the mouse pointer onto the area of a slide show, the **Slide Show Controls** are displayed, as shown in Fig. 3.24 below. These have the following functions.

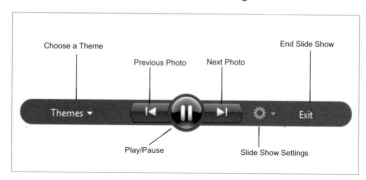

Fig. 3.24 The Slide Show Controls

Themes display your photos in different ways, with some filling the screen with one picture and others arranging several on the screen at once.

The **Slide Show Settings** button gives you control over the **Speed** of the slide show, lets you **Shuffle** its order, **Loop** to play it continuously, and **Mute** to switch off any sound effects.

To end the **Slide Show**, click the **Exit** button on the controls, or press the **Esc** key.

4

Using the Internet

How did we ever manage without the Internet? It links many millions of computers around the world and has revolutionised how we get information and use our computers. Maybe the two things most people use the Internet for, are browsing the Web and e-mail.

The Web (or World Wide Web in full) consists of millions of web sites which give a magazine like view of almost everything you can think of, but with sound and video as well.

Once you are connected to the Internet you can send e-mail messages to anyone with an e-mail address anywhere in the world. It's free and almost instant. No wonder it's so popular. If you are like us, almost the first thing you do in the morning is check your e-mail!

As you would expect, Vista comes well equipped for the Internet. Once you have a connection, you can access the Web using Internet Explorer, and do your e-mailing with Windows Mail, both included with Vista.

Internet Explorer

 To start **Internet Explorer**, either click its icon 🅮 on the **Quick Launch** bar (page 6), or click **Start**, **All Programs**, and select **Internet Explorer** 🅮 Internet Explorer from the **Start** menu. Either of these options, opens Vista's Internet browser. The first time you do this, you will probably be stepped through the process of establishing a connection to the Internet.

There are three ways of doing this; **Wireless**, **Broadband**, or **Dial-up**. For a **Wireless** connection you need a wireless router or a network. For a **Broadband** connection you need a broadband modem, also called DSL (Digital Subscriber Line), or a cable modem. For the slowest option, a **Dial-up** connection, you will need a modem, but most computers come with a 56 Kbps modem already installed.

Fig. 4.1 Starting Connection Setup

Whichever method you select you will need to subscribe to an ISP (Internet Service Provider) and you might have to purchase extra hardware. Normally, ISPs provide you with a CD which automates the setup process, but you could also use the **Tools** toolbar icon in Internet Explorer, select **Internet Options** from the drop-down menu and click the **Setup** button on the Connections tab sheet, as shown here in Fig. 4.1.

However, before starting this operation be sure to find out from your Internet Service Provider (ISP), exactly what settings you will need to enter. They will usually send you a letter with these details, if not you will need to phone them.

The first time you manage to access the Web you will probably get a page supplied by Microsoft or your Service Provider. But you can control what Web page is displayed when you start **Explorer** (called your Home page), in the **General** settings sheet opened with the **Tools**, **Internet Options** menu command. Select **Use Current** to make any currently open page your home page, or **Use Blank** to show a clear window whenever you start **Explorer**.

Searching the Web

There are many millions of Web pages to look at on the Web, so where do you start? Our favourite place to start is with Google, so let's take a quick look. Start **Explorer**, if it is not already going, log onto the Internet, then type **www.google.co.uk** into the **Address** bar (see Fig. 4.3), and press the **Enter** key on the keyboard, or click the **Go to** button ➔ to the right of the address bar.

Fig. 4.2 The Google UK Search Page

If all is well and your connection is good you should see Google UK's search page, as in Fig. 4.2. Bear in mind that this (and other Web site screens in the book) may be different at the time you access them. Google especially, like to change their opening logos for special events. The one above was to celebrate the Queen's visit to one of their offices.

Moving the mouse over the underlined links, and some graphics on the page, changes the pointer to a hand 🖑. Clicking the hand pointer, jumps you to different parts of the Web site, or to other sites. This is how the Web works.

The Address Bar

In Internet Explorer the Address Bar, shown below, is where you type, or paste, the address or URL (Universal Resource Locator, a fancy term for Web page address) of a Web page you want to open.

Fig. 4.3 The Address Bar

This will open the Web page shown in Fig. 4.2 when the **Go to** button → is clicked. Note that the **Go to** button then changes to the **Refresh** button which reloads the Web page shown in the **Address** bar when it is clicked.

Fig. 4.4 Drop-down Menu

The **Address** bar is the main way of opening new Web pages when you know their URLs. A drop-down menu of the most recent locations you have entered, can be opened by clicking the black down-arrow at the right of the address box.

The status bar, at the bottom of the screen (Fig. 4.5), shows the URL address of the link pointed to and the loading progress of the Web page in question.

Fig. 4.5 The Status Bar

Explorer Buttons

As with other Vista windows, **Internet Explorer** is fully equipped with a toolbar (command bar), with buttons you can left-click to quickly carry out a program function.

Fig. 4.6 The Internet Explorer Toolbar

Most of the buttons are pretty self-explanatory and have the following functions:

Button	*Function*
Back	Displays the previous page viewed. If there isn't one this is 'greyed out'.
Forward	Displays the next page on the **History** list, or is 'greyed out'.
Recent	Opens a drop-menu of recent pages you have visited.
Refresh	Brings a fresh copy of the current Web page to the browser.
Stop	Halts any on-line transfer of page data.
Search	Searches for the text typed into the **Search** box.
Favorites	Opens the **Favorites Center** from which you can choose the **Favorites**, **Feeds** or **History** bars.
Add to	Adds a favourite site to the **Favorites** bar.
Quick Tabs	Displays all the currently active sites as thumbnails in one window.
New Tab	Allows you to load another Web site into the current Explorer window. More about this shortly.
Home	Displays your specified home page, with a Microsoft page as the default.
Feeds	View Feeds on this Web site. If a feed is not detected the colour of the icon remains grey.
Print	Prints the open Web page, or frame, using the current print settings.
Page	Opens a menu that allows you to open a new window, save the current page,

send it or a link to it by e-mail, zoom the page, or change the text size on it.

Tools   Displays a drop-down menu that allows you to delete the browsing **History**, manage pop-ups, set 'phishing' filters, work offline, specify your Internet options, and generally control how Internet Explorer works.

Help   Opens a drop-down menu giving quick access to **Help** topics.

Blog This   Opens Windows Live Writer to create or add content to your blog.

Research   Allows you to carry out research into a specific subject.

Fig. 4.7 Sub-menu

Clicking the **Tools** button and selecting **Toolbars,** opens the sub-menu shown in Fig. 4.7. With the **Customize** option you can control what buttons display on the bar, by adding or removing them in the **Customize Toolbar** box (Fig. 4.8). You can also open **Favorites**, **History**, or **Feeds** panes from here.

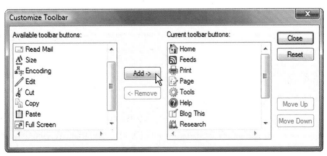

Fig. 4.8 The Customize Toolbar Box

Favorites

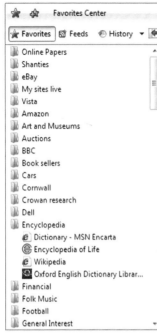

Fig. 4.9 Favorites Centre

Using Favorites, or Bookmarks, is an easy way to save Web page addresses for future use. It's much easier to select a page from a sorted list, than to manually type a URL address into the Address field. You don't have to remember the address and are less likely to make a typing error!

With **Internet Explorer** your Favorites are kept in the **Favorites Center**, shown here, opened by clicking the **Favorites** button 📄.

To keep the list open in a separate pane, you click the **Pin the Favorites Center** button 📄. To close it again, click its **Close** button ☒.

Adding a Favorite – There are several ways to add a 'Favorite' to your list. When you are viewing a Web page that you want to visit again, right-click in the page and select **Add to Favorites** from the context menu. Another way is to click the **Add to Favorites** button 📄 and select the **Add to Favorites** menu option, or you can use the **Ctrl+D** shortcut.

Fig. 4.10 The Add a Favorite Box

All of these methods open the Add a Favorite dialogue box (Fig. 4.10) in which you can give the new Favorite a name, and choose a folder to put it in. Then just click the **Add** button to finish.

Browsing History

Fig. 4.11 Browsing History

Internet Explorer stores details of all the Web pages and files you view on your hard disc, and places temporary pointers to them in a folder. To return to these in the future, click the **View History** button in the **Favorites Center**, to open the **History** list shown in Fig. 4.11.

In this list you can see what Web sites you visited in the last 3 weeks. Clicking a listed site opens links to the individual Web pages you went to. Clicking any of these will open the page again.

The length of time history items are kept on your hard disc can be set by clicking the **Tools** button and selecting

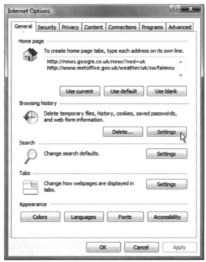

Fig. 4.12 General Internet Options

Internet Options to open the tabbed dialogue box shown in Fig. 4.12.

Clicking the **Settings** button in the **Browsing history** section opens an additional dialogue box in which you can select the number of days that **History** files are kept (between 0 and 999). To delete all history items click the **Delete** button, which will release the hard disc space used.

Web Feeds

Web feeds (feeds for short) are usually used for news and blogs and contain frequently updated content published by a Web site. You can use feeds if you want updates to a Web site to be automatically downloaded to your PC.

When you visit a Web page that contains feeds, the grey **Feeds** button on the Internet Explorer toolbar changes to orange. To look at the feed, click the feed symbol. To get its content automatically downloaded to your computer, you will need to subscribe to the feed. This is very easy to do, and doesn't cost anything! Just clicking a **Subscribe to this feed** link, like that shown in Fig. 4.13, adds your selection to the 'Common Feed List' in the **Favorites Center**, and updated information from the feed will be automatically down-loaded to your computer for viewing in Internet Explorer.

Fig. 4.13 Subscribing to a Web Feed

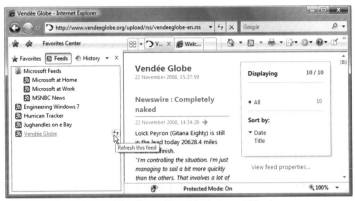

Fig. 4.14 Viewing a Feed in Internet Explorer

All your subscribed feeds will be listed in the **Feeds** section of the **Favorites Center** as shown in Fig. 4.14. Clicking an item will open it in the right pane so you can keep up to date.

Tabbed Browsing

With tabbed browsing you can open several Web sites in one Explorer window each in its own tab, and switch between them by clicking on their tab. To create a new tab, click the **New Tab** icon , pointed to in Fig. 4.15, immediately to the right of the existing tabs, or use the **Ctrl+T** shortcut.

Fig. 4.15 Creating a New Tab

The first time you do this, a special tabbed browsing information page opens as shown in Fig. 4.16 below.

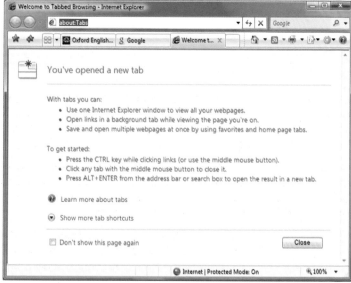

Fig. 4.16 The Welcome to Tabbed Browsing Page

Please read the above text, and note that the 'link' **about:Tabs** is highlighted in the Address Bar so you can simply type a new Web address, or click the **Favorites** button and open one of your **Favorites**.

The active tab is a darker colour and has an **Close** button ⌧ after its name, which can be clicked to close the tab.

Using Quick Tabs – When you have several Web sites open in different tabs a new button appears between the first tab and the **Add to Favorites** button. This is the **Quick Tabs** button ⊞ which displays all the tabbed Web sites as thumbnail images when it is clicked, as shown in Fig. 4.17.

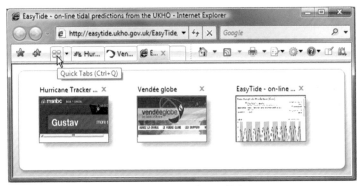

Fig. 4.17 Using Quick Tabs

In this view you can click a thumbnail to open its Web page, or click the **Close Tab** button ⌧ on a thumbnail to close the Web page. Clicking the **Quick Tabs** button again closes the thumbnails and opens the last Web page you were viewing.

Saving and Opening a Group of Tabs – To save a group of tabs, click the **Add to Favorites** button ⭐, select **Add Tab Group to Favorites** from the displayed list, give the group a name (as in Fig. 4.10) and click the **Add** button.

Fig. 4.18 Opening a Tabbed Group

To open a group of tabs, click the **Favorites** button ⭐, select the group folder you want to open, and click the arrow to the right of the folder name ➡ to open all the tabbed sites in the group.

Internet Explorer Help

Contents and Index

Internet Explorer Tour
Online Support
Send Feedback

About Internet Explorer

Fig. 4.19

That's all we have space for on **Internet Explorer**, but don't forget the built-in **Help** system if you want to go deeper. It is accessed by clicking the **Help** toolbar button and selecting the **Contents and Index** option from the drop-down menu as shown in Fig. 4.19.

This opens a Windows Help and Support window. To show a list of contents click the **Browse Help** button ▢.

Another way of browsing the **Help** system is to use its **Search** facility to find specific topics. In Fig. 4.20 below we searched for help on Internet Explorer!

Fig. 4.20 Searching the Help System

You can also access product support from Microsoft with the **Online Support** option shown in Fig. 4.19 above, or click the **Online Help** button ● Online Help ▾ at the bottom of the Help window itself.

5

Using E-mail

 Once you are connected to the Internet and set up correctly you can communicate with others by e-mail (electronic mail). Wherever they are in the World, all you need to know is their e-mail address. In this chapter we look at Windows Mail, the e-mail program that comes with Windows Vista, but you can use another program if you prefer.

Windows Mail

A shortcut to Windows Mail should already have been added to the **Start** menu of your PC, so clicking the **Start** button ●, and clicking the 📧 **Windows Mail** shortcut entry will open the program. Otherwise find and click it in the **All Programs** menu (see page 12).

Fig. 5.1 The Windows Mail Window

Connecting to your Server

Before you can send or receive e-mails you have to establish a connection to your ISP's (Internet Service Provider) e-mail servers. You will need the following information from the supplier of your e-mail service. Your e-mail address and password, the type of e-mail server to be used, and the address of the incoming and outgoing e-mail servers you should use.

If the connection process does not start automatically, use the **Tools**, **Accounts** menu command, pointed to in Fig. 5.1, to start it manually. In the Internet Accounts dialogue box that opens, click the **Add** button and in the next screen select **E-mail Account**, and click **Next** and follow the instructions from screen to screen. It should only take a couple of minutes. For more details on this you can search Vista **Help** (see page 26) for **Windows Mail: Setting up an account from start to finish**.

Once your connection is established, opening the **Inbox** will display any messages waiting in your mailbox, as shown in Fig. 5.2 below.

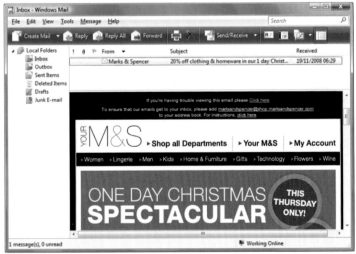

Fig. 5.2 A Message in the Windows Mail Window

This shows the default Windows Mail main window layout, which consists of a **Folders List** to the left, a set of toolbar buttons, including ones for **Contacts** and **Windows Calendar**, a **Message List** in the top right of the screen, and a **Preview** pane below that. The list under **Folders** contains all the active mail folders, news servers and newsgroups. Clicking on one of these, displays its contents in the **Message List**. Clicking on a message in the list opens a preview of it, while double-clicking on a message opens the message in its own window.

To check your mail at any time, click the **Send/Recv** toolbar button ![Send/Receive] which, if you have an 'always on' Broadband connection will automatically download your messages. If you are using a Dial-up connection, it will display the Dial-up Connection window, and you will have to click the **Connect** button to connect to the Internet. Any new messages will then be downloaded from your mailbox.

A Test E-mail Message

Before explaining in more detail the main features of **Windows Mail** we will step through the procedure of sending a very simple e-mail message. The best way to test out any unfamiliar e-mail features is to send a test message to your own e-mail address. This saves wasting somebody else's time, and the message can be very quickly checked.

To start, click the **Create Mail** icon ![Create Mail] to open the New Message window, shown in Fig. 5.3.

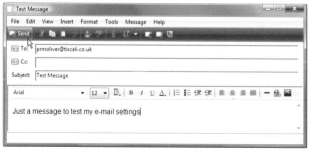

Fig. 5.3 Creating a Test Message

Type your own e-mail address in the **To:** field, and a title for the message in the **Subject:** field. The text in this subject field will form a header for the message when it is received, so it helps to show in a few words what the message is about. Next, type your message in the main body of the window and click the **Send** button .

By default, your message is placed in the **Outbox** folder and sent immediately if you are on Broadband, otherwise you will have to press the **Send/Recv** button ![Send/Receive] to connect to the Internet and send it.

If all is well, when **Windows Mail** next checks for mail, it will find the message and download it into the **Inbox** folder.

The Main Window

Windows Mail uses three windows, which we will refer to as: the Main window which opens first; the Read Message window for reading your mail; and the New Message window, to compose your outgoing mail messages.

The Main window consists of a toolbar, a menu, and three panes with the default display shown in our example in Fig. 5.2. You can choose different pane layouts, and customise the toolbar, with the **View**, **Layout** menu command, but we will let you try these for yourself.

The Folders List – The **Folders** pane contains a list of your mail folders, your news servers and any newsgroups you have subscribed to. There are always at least six mail folders, as shown in Fig. 5.4 below. You can add your own with the **File**, **Folder**, **New** menu command from the Main window. You can delete added folders with the **File**, **Folder**, **Delete** command. These operations can also be carried out after right-clicking a folder in the list. You can drag messages from the **Message** list and drop them into any of the folders, to 'store' them there.

Local Folders
- Inbox
- Outbox
- Sent Items
- Deleted Items
- Drafts
- Junk E-mail

Fig. 5.4 The Local Folders Pane

The Message List – When you select a folder, by clicking it in the **Folders** list, the **Message** list shows the contents of that folder. Brief details of each message are displayed on one line, as shown in Fig. 5.5 below.

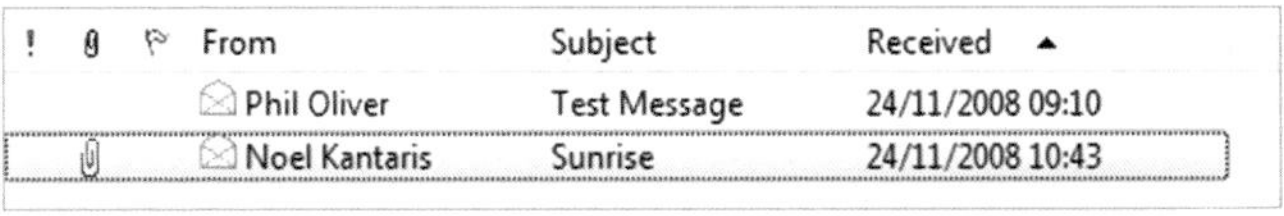

!	❀	↦	From	Subject	Received ▲
			✉ Phil Oliver	Test Message	24/11/2008 09:10
	ⓤ		✉ Noel Kantaris	Sunrise	24/11/2008 10:43

Fig. 5.5 Received Messages in Ascending Date Order

The first column shows the message priority, if any, the second whether the message has an attachment, and the third whether the message has been 'flagged'. All of these are indicated by icons on the message line.

The 'From' column shows the name of the sender, 'Subject' shows the title of each e-mail message, and 'Received' shows the date and time it reached you. You can control what columns display in this pane with the **View**, **Columns** menu command.

To sort a list of messages, you can click the mouse pointer in the title of the column you want the list sorted on, clicking it again will sort it in reverse order. The sorted column is shown with a triangle mark, as shown in both Fig. 5.5 and 5.6.

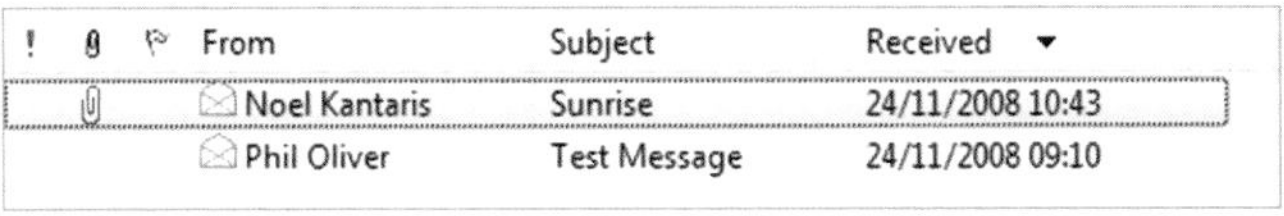

!	❀	↦	From	Subject	Received ▼
	ⓤ		✉ Noel Kantaris	Sunrise	24/11/2008 10:43
			✉ Phil Oliver	Test Message	24/11/2008 09:10

Fig. 5.6 Received Messages in Descending Date Order

This shows our preferred method of display with the received messages sorted by date, with the most recent message at the top.

The Preview Pane – When you select a message in the **Message** list, by clicking it once, it is displayed in the **Preview** pane below, which takes up the rest of the window. This lets you read the first few lines to see if the message is worth bothering with.

If it is worth reading, double-clicking the header in the **Message** list, will open the message in the Read Message window, as shown later in the chapter.

You can use the **Preview** pane to read all your mail, especially if your messages are on the short side, but it is easier to process them from the Read Message window.

The Main Window Toolbar

Selecting any one of the local folders displays the following buttons on Windows Mail's toolbar.

 Opens the New Message window for creating a new mail message, with the **To:** field blank.

 Opens the New Message window for replying to the current mail message, with the **To:** field pre-addressed to the original sender. The original **Subject** field is prefixed with **Re:**.

 Opens the New Message window for replying to the current mail message, with the **To:** field pre-addressed to all that received copies of the original message. The original **Subject** field is prefixed with **Re:**.

 Opens the New Message window for forwarding the current mail message. The **To:** field is blank. The original **Subject** field is prefixed with **Fw:**.

 Prints the selected message.

 Deletes the currently selected message and places it in the **Deleted Items** folder.

 Connects to the mailbox server and downloads waiting messages, which it places in the **Inbox** folder. Sends any messages waiting in the **Outbox** folder.

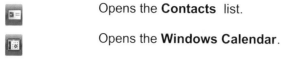

Opens the **Contacts** list.

Opens the **Windows Calendar**.

Finds a message or an e-mail address using the **Find People** facility of the **Contacts** list.

Toggles the **Folders** list on or off.

The Read Message Window

If you double-click a message in the **Message** list of the Main window, the Read Message window is opened as shown in Fig. 5.7 below.

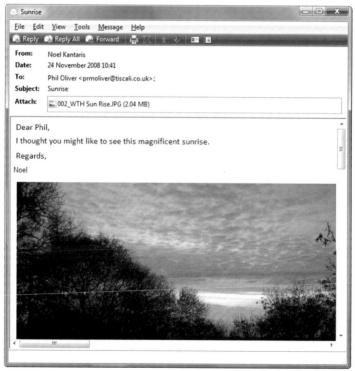

Fig. 5.7 The Read Message Window

This is the best window to read your mail in. It has its own menu system and toolbar, which lets you rapidly process and move between the messages in a folder. Only two icons are different in this window's toolbar from those in the Main window.

 Previous – Displays the previous mail message in the Read Message window.

 Next – Displays the next mail message in the Read Message window.

These buttons give an audible warning if there are no previous or further messages.

The New Message Window

This is the window, shown in Fig. 5.8, that you use to create your e-mail messages in Windows Mail. It is important to understand its features, so that you can get the most out of it.

Fig. 5.8 The New Message Window

As we saw, this window can be opened by using the **Create Mail** toolbar icon from the Main window, as well as the **Message**, **New Message** menu command.

From other windows you can also use the **Message**, **New** menu command. The newly opened window has its own menu system and toolbar, which let you rapidly prepare and send your e-mail messages.

The Message Toolbar

The icons on the New Message window toolbar have the following functions:

 Send – Sends message, either to the recipient, or to the **Outbox** folder.

 Cut – Cuts selected text to the Windows **Clipboard**.

 Copy – Copies selected text to the Windows **Clipboard**.

 Paste – Pastes the contents of the Windows **Clipboard** into the current message.

 Undo – Undoes the last editing action.

 Check Names – Checks that names match your entries in the **Contacts** list, or are in correct e-mail address format.

 Spelling – Checks the spelling of the current message before it is sent, but is only available if you have **Word**, **Excel**, or **PowerPoint**.

 Attach File – Opens the Insert Attachment window for you to select a file to be attached to the current message.

 Set Priority – Sets the message priority as high or low, to indicate its importance to the recipient.

 Sign Message – Adds a digital signature to the message to confirm to the recipient that it is from you.

 Encrypt Message – Encodes the message so that only the recipient can read it.

 Offline – Closes a Dial-up connection to the Internet so that you can process your mail offline. The button then changes to **Work Online.**

Message Formatting

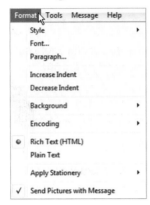

Windows Mail provides quite sophisticated formatting options for an e-mail editor from both the **Format** menu and toolbar. These only work if you prepare the message in HTML format, as used in Web documents. You can set this to be your default mail sending format using the Send tab in the **Tools**, **Options** box of the Read Message window.

Fig. 5.9 The Format Sub-menu.

To use the format for the current message only, select **Rich Text (HTML)** from the **Format** menu, as we have done here. If **Plain Text** is selected, the blue dot will be placed against this option on the menu, and the formatting features will not then be available.

The **Format** toolbar shown in Fig. 5.10 below is added to the New Message window when you are in HTML mode and all the **Format** menu options are then made active.

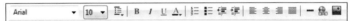

Fig. 5.10 The Format Toolbar.

As all the formatting features are self-explanatory, we will not delve into them here. You should be able to prepare some very easily readable e-mail messages with these features, but remember that not everyone will be able to read the work in the way that you spent hours creating. When your recipient's e-mail program does not read HTML, and many people set theirs not to, the message appears as plain text with an HTML file attached.

Replying to a Message

When you receive an e-mail message that you want to reply to, Windows Mail makes it very easy to do. The reply address and the new message subject fields are both added automatically for you. Also, by default, the original message is quoted in the reply window for you to edit as required.

With the message you want to reply to still open, click the **Reply** toolbar button [Reply] to open the New Message window and the message you are replying to will, by default, be placed under the insertion point.

With long messages, you should not leave all of the original text in your reply. This can be bad practice, which rapidly makes new messages very large and time consuming to download. You should usually edit the quoted text, so that it is obvious what you are referring to. Just a few lines may well be enough.

Deleting Messages

Most messages you receive will need deleting after you have read them. From the Read Message window you just click the **Delete** button [×] to do this. From the Main window you can select the messages you don't want to keep in the Messages List pane and either, click the **Delete** button [×], or press the **Delete** key.

Whenever you delete a message it is actually moved to the **Deleted Items** folder. If ignored, this folder gets bigger and bigger over time, so you need to check it frequently and manually re-delete messages you are sure you will not need again.

To get this done automatically, you use the **Tools**, **Options** menu command on the Read Message window to open the Options dialogue box, click the Advance tab and click the **Maintenance** button at the bottom of the screen and check the **Empty messages from the 'Deleted Items' folder on exit** box in the displayed Maintenance screen. Your deletions will then be fully removed whenever you close the Windows Mail program.

E-mail Attachments

To add an attachment to an e-mail message, such as a photo or work file, you simply click the **Attach File** toolbar button ▪ in the New Message window which shows the Vista standard Open dialogue box, shown in Fig. 5.11, for you to select the file(s), you want to go with your message, and click **Open**.

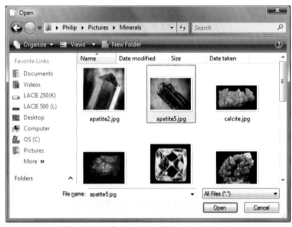

Fig. 5.11 Selecting Files to Attach

In **Windows Mail** the attached files are placed below the **Subject** box. In Fig. 5.12 we show two attachments with their icons telling the recipient what each file is; a graphics (**.jpg**) file and a Notepad (**.txt**) text file in our case.

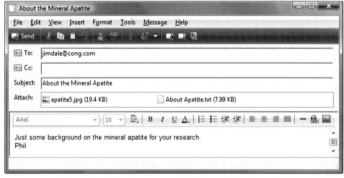

Fig. 5.12 A Message with Two Attachments

Clicking the **Send** button 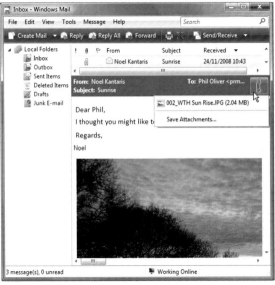 on the toolbar, transfers the message (with its attachments, if any) to the **Outbox** folder, and with broadband sends it straight away. With a dial-up connection, the next time you click the **Send/Recv** button, Windows Mail connects to your ISP and sends all the e-mail messages in the **Outbox**.

Receiving Attachments

Fig. 5.13 below shows a received e-mail with an attachment in a Main window view.

Fig. 5.13 A Received E-mail with an Attachment

The received message shows the graphics (**.jpg**) file open at the bottom of the **Preview** pane, and the **Attach** icon in the Header bar indicating that the message has attachments.

To find out how many attachments were included with the message, left-click the **Attach** icon to open a drop-down list as shown in Fig. 5.13. From here you can also choose to save the attachment to a selected folder.

Left-clicking a graphics file (**.jpg**) opens it in **Windows Photo Gallery**, while left-clicking a document file opens a Mail Attachment window showing you the type of document and asking whether you want to open it.

Each document file can be opened in situ or saved to disc from within the application that opened it.

Spell Checking Messages

Just because e-mail messages are a quick way of getting in touch with friends and family, there is no reason why they should be full of spelling mistakes. Windows Mail is linked to the spell checker that comes with other Microsoft programs. If you do not have any of these, the option will be greyed out.

To try it out, prepare a message in the New Message window, but make an obvious spelling mistake, maybe like ours below. Pressing the **Spelling** toolbar button █, or using the **Tools, Spelling** menu command, opens the Spelling box shown in Fig. 5.14 below.

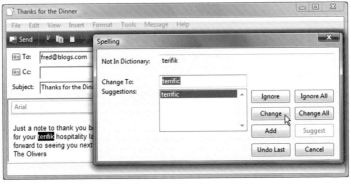

Fig. 5.14 Checking the Spelling of a Message

Any words not recognised by the spell checker will be flagged up as shown. If you are happy with the word just click one of the **Ignore** buttons, if not, you can type a correction in the **Change To** field, or accept one of the **Suggestions** before clicking the **Change** button. The **Add** option adds your original word to the dictionary.

Printing Messages

Windows Mail lets you print e-mail messages to paper, but it doesn't give you any control over the page settings it uses. You can, however, alter the font size of your printed output as it depends on the font size you set for viewing your messages. With the **View**, **Text Size** menu command in the Read Message window you have five 'relative' size options to choose from.

When you are ready to print a message which is open in the Read Message window, or selected in the Message List of the Main window, click the **Print** toolbar button 🖶, use the **Ctrl+P** key combination, or the **File**, **Print** menu command. All of these open the standard Vista Print dialogue box which allows you to select one of your printers, the **Page Range**, and **Number of copies** you want. Clicking the **Print** button will send the message to paper.

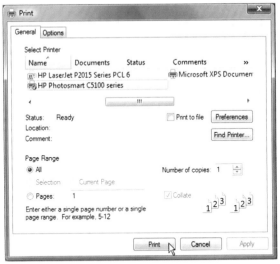

Fig. 5.15 The Print Dialogue Box

The Contacts Folder

With Vista you can keep track of people and organisations by creating 'contacts' for them in **Windows Contacts**, which places a Contacts folder in your personal folders list, containing such things as names, addresses, e-mail details, fax and phone numbers, etc. This folder is used as the address book for Windows Mail, so when you create an e-mail message in Windows Mail, you can select the recipient from your Contacts folder.

To access the **Contacts** folder, use the **Start**, **All Programs**, **Windows Contacts** menu command, or from inside Windows Mail, you just click the **Contacts** button ![icon].

Fig. 5.16 The Windows Contacts Folder

Here in Fig. 5.16 we show a small part of a **Contacts** folder. Once in **Windows Contacts**, you can add a person's details in a new Properties dialogue box opened by clicking the **New Contact** button ![New Contact]. This opens the window shown in Fig. 5.17 on the facing page.

Use the Name and E-mail tab to enter the name, title, and e-mail address for your new contact. The Home tab screen is used to enter her address, telephone, Fax number, and Web site. You can also enter similar information for Work. The rest of the information can be entered if you have the time, or be entered later by editing the Contact's entry.

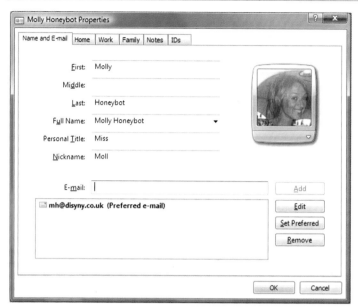

Fig. 5.17 A Contact's Properties Dialogue Box

To send a new message to anyone listed in your **Contacts** list, open **Windows Mail**, click the **Create Mail** button to open the New Message window, click on either of the **To:** or **Cc:** buttons, or use the **Tools**, **Select Recipients** command, to open the Select Recipients dialogue box.

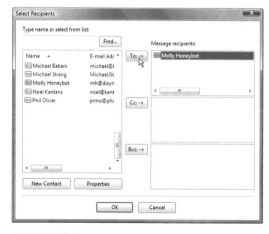

Fig. 5.18 Select Recipients Box

In this box, you can select a person's name and click either the **To:** button to place it in the **To** field of your message, the **Cc:** button to place it in the **Copy** field, or the **Bcc:** button to place it in the **B**lind Copy field.

The Windows Calendar

Vista also provides you with a calendar which you can open with the **Start**, **All Programs**, **Windows Calendar** menu command, or from Windows Mail by clicking the **Calendar** button 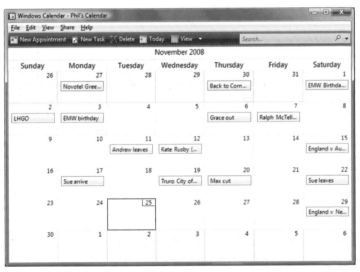.

Fig. 5.19 The Windows Calendar

This will provide you with all the scheduling tools you should ever need. It provides day, working week, week and month views, includes a to-do list and supports multiple, colour-coded calendars, making it easy to keep schedules for work, family, school and hobbies, etc.

We will leave it to you to explore this excellent facility on your own.

6

Keeping your PC Healthy

Vista comes equipped with a full range of utilities for you to easily maintain your PC's health and well-being. You can access most of these tools by selecting **System Tools** from the **Start**, **All Programs**, **Accessories** menu, which opens the group of options shown in Fig. 6.1 below.

Fig. 6.1 System Tools

Quite an impressive list, but of all the available tools, **System Information** is the easiest to take a first look at – it displays such things as your Operating System, System Summary, Hardware Resources, etc. As each one of these is bound to be different for different PCs, we leave it to you to examine the information for your own system.

Problem Prevention

Vista provides threefold protection against System corruption:

- System Protection
- Automatic Update
- System Restore

These will be discussed shortly, but now might be a good time to copy your data to a DVD or external hard drive, as discussed in Chapter 3. After all, hard discs do 'crash' and your PC could be stolen, or lost in a fire, or flood. Any of these events would cause a serious data loss, so it's a good idea to have copies stored away safely.

System Protection

Windows applications sometimes can, and do, overwrite important **System** files. The Business, Enterprise and Ultimate versions of Vista protect your **System** files by automatically restoring them to their original version, if any changes have been attempted by an application program.

Automatic Update

Fig. 6.2 Selecting Windows Update

Vista can automatically update any **System** files as they become available from the Microsoft Web site. To make sure this happens, click **Start, All Programs**, and select the **Windows Update** menu option, shown here in Fig. 6.2, and you will be connected to Microsoft's Web site.

Click the **Check for updates** link on the left panel to get a list of updates for your system, (Fig. 6.3). Then click the **View available updates** link on the right of the window and select which ones you need. There is no point downloading updates that have no relevance to you. Finally clicking the **Install Updates** button (Fig. 6.3) will start the updating process.

It is important to keep Vista, your PC operating system, as up to date as possible to make sure that as security issues are found and corrected by Microsoft they are installed on your system straight away. We recommend you click the **Change settings** link (second on the list of links on the left panel) and make sure the **Install updates automatically** option is selected, as recommended by Microsoft. This should guarantee you are always up to date.

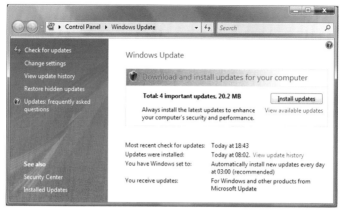

Fig. 6.3 Checking for Windows Updates

System Restore

 System Restore automatically backs up Vista's registry and system files whenever you install new software or drivers, and enables you to restore your computer to an earlier state without losing any of your data files (such as e-mails, documents, or photos). You would typically use System Restore if your computer starts misbehaving after an update or a new software installation. Restoring your PC to an earlier restore point may well resolve the problem.

Note – Software (programs) installed since the restore point was made will be removed from your PC.

Every time you start to install a new program, System Restore takes a snapshot of your system before starting the installation. You can also force System Restore to take a snapshot at any other time.

To examine the utility, click the **Start** button 🔵, type **restore** in the search field, and select 🔲 System Restore from the resulting list. Or use the **Start, All Programs, Accessories, System Tools** menu command and select **System Restore**. Both methods open the window shown in Fig. 6.4 on the next page.

Fig. 6.4 The System Restore Opening Window

As you can see, from this window you can select to undo the most recent update by clicking **Next**, or **Choose a different restore point**, or create a new restore point by clicking the **open System Protection** link. We chose the second option to restore our computer to an earlier time and clicked the **Next** button. This displayed a further window, as shown in Fig. 6.5 below.

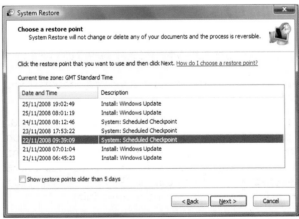

Fig. 6.5 Our Recent Available System Restore Points

Selecting a restore point from the list and clicking **Next**, starts the **Restore** process, then you just follow the instructions. Once the restore has started you shouldn't stop your computer, or you might end up in trouble.

To create a new restore point, click the **open System Protection** link (Fig. 6.4), to display the window below, if necessary select other hard discs, and click the **Create** button.

Fig. 6.6 Setting a New System Restore Point

Our two external hard drives above only contain data, not system files, so were not selected.

If things go really wrong with your system and Vista won't even start, you can try starting your computer from the installation DVD, and choose the **Repair your computer** option on the lower left side on the menu. This will let you choose **System Restore** from the System Recovery dialogue box. Hopefully you will never have to do this!

The Windows Security Center

 To examine the options available in the Windows **Security Center**, click the **Start** button ⬤, **Control Panel**, then double-click the icon, shown on the left, to display the window in Fig. 6.7 below.

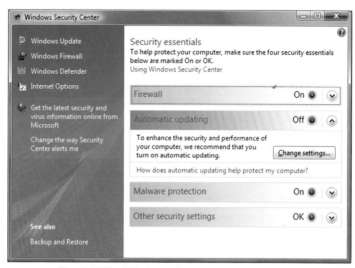

Fig. 6.7 The Windows Security Centre Window

For your PC to be secure, the four items here should show a green light ⬤ and be either **On** or **OK**. When something is wrong, a red light ⬤ shows, and you are pointed in the right direction to solve the problem, as above.

A **Firewall** is a software security system that sits between your computer and the outside world and is used to set restrictions on what information is passed to and from the Internet. In other words it protects you from uninvited outside access. **Malware protection** checks your computer to see if you are using up-to-date antivirus and antispyware programs to protect against malicious software. If these are turned off, or are out of date, **Security Center** will warn you and put a warning icon ⊗ in the notification area of the Taskbar.

Disk Cleanup

 Disk Cleanup locates and removes unnecessary files on your computer which can help you free up space on your hard drive(s). To start it, click the **Start** button ●, type **cleanup** in the search field, and select  from the resulting list. Or use the **Start**, **All Programs**, **Accessories**, **System Tools** command and click the **Disk Cleanup** entry.

Fig. 6.8 Choosing the Files to Clean Up

The first thing that **Disk Cleanup** does is to ask you to select which files to clean up, as shown in Fig. 6.8, then it asks you which drive you want to clean up. It then scans the drive, and lists temporary files, Internet cache files, and other files that you can safely delete, as shown in Fig. 6.9 below.

Fig. 6.9 Files Found that can be Cleaned Up

As you can see, we could free quite a bit of disc space by deleting all the files selected (4.06GB), and even more (6.06GB) by deleting the **Hibernation File Cleaner** as well. Please **do not proceed** with the latter deletion, though, until you read the small print in Fig. 6.9, which is displayed after highlighting the **Hibernation File Cleaner** entry.

If you activate the **Hibernation File Cleaner** (by selecting it in the list) your PC will lose the ability to **Hibernate** (see page 14), and getting it back can be a bit complicated. Of course, if you don't use hibernation there is no problem.

Fig. 6.10 Cleaning a Disc

In our case we selected everything else on the list, clicked the **OK** button, and watched the green progress bar (Fig. 6.10) as the disc was cleaned of useless files.

Defragmenting your Hard Discs

The **Disk Defragmenter** optimises your hard discs by rearranging their data to eliminate unused spaces, which speeds up access by all of Windows' operations. These days you don't even need to close running applications before starting **Disk Defragmenter**.

To start the process, click the **Start** button ●, type **defrag** in the search field, and select ⬚ Disk Defragmenter from the resulting list. The utility then takes a few minutes to scan and analyse your hard discs. If necessary, choose which drive you want to defragment and click the **Defragment Now** button.

You can defragment a drive in the background by minimising the window to the **Taskbar**. Vista does not show the operation on screen, unless you like watching a small circle going around and around for a few hours! In fact, you get no messages at all from the defragmenter, not even when it finishes the process, except for the focus on the default button changing from **Cancel defragmentation** to ● .

Backing up your Data

 Anyone can lose files by: accidentally deleting or replacing them, a virus attack, a software or hardware failure, or a complete hard disc failure. With Vista, you can use **System Restore** to recover your system (or Vista) files, you can re-install your programs, but what about your precious data files? To protect these, you should regularly create backups, or sets of copies of your data files, stored in a different location from the original files.

Too many people don't think about backing up their data until it has already been lost! Please don't let this happen to you. Vista makes backing up easier, and has a range of features to seamlessly protect your data.

- **File Backup**, using the **Back Up Files** wizard, is available in most editions of Vista (manually only in Home Basic). This is the Backup we describe here.

- **Complete PC Backup** performs a complete, image-based backup of your entire computer. Unfortunately, this is only available in the Business, Ultimate, and Enterprise editions of Vista, so we will not look at it.

You should regularly back up the files you create and modify. With the **Back Up Files** wizard, this can be done automatically once you have set it up (except with Vista Home Basic). It's also a good idea to back up your data files before making any major system changes, such as adding new hardware, updating drivers, editing the registry, or making large changes to Windows, such as installing a service pack.

The Backup and Restore Center

This is where you carry out all your backups. You can open this from the **Control Panel** but the easiest way is to click the **Start** button 🔵, type **backup** in the search field, and select 🔲 Backup and Restore Center from the resulting list. With Vista Home Premium edition, this opens as in Fig. 6.11.

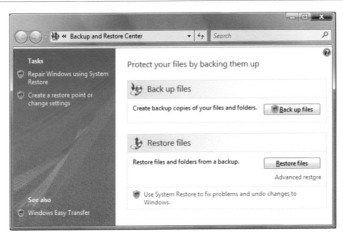

Fig. 6.11 The Backup and Restore Centre

When you click the **Back up files** button, a User Account Control (UAC) dialogue box opens, you should click the **Continue** button to confirm you started the procedure.

The Back Up Files window, shown in Fig. 6.12, opens next in which you are prompted to select the location to save your backup.

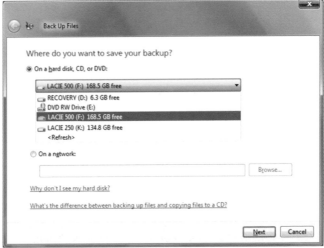

Fig. 6.12 Selecting Where to Save Your Backup

The **Back Up Files** wizard can save backups to a DVD (or CD) burning drive, a network drive, or a secondary internal or external hard drive. It doesn't support tape or flash drives, and you can't back up to the drive Vista is installed on.

The ideal destination is an external hard disc attached to a USB port on your PC. We show two in Fig. 6.12. With this arrangement it is much less hassle automating the backup procedure. Make your selection and click the **Next** button.

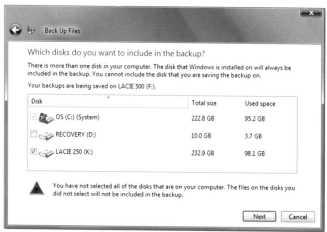

Fig. 6.13 Selecting Discs to Include in the Backup

The next window (Fig. 6.13), contains a list of all your active hard discs and partitions except the one you selected as the destination of your backup. Where Vista is installed is selected by default, usually the C: drive. You can choose to include or exclude drives from the backup procedure. In Fig. 6.13 we excluded our D: drive as it is not used for data storage. Make your selection and click the **Next** button again.

The wizard then asks you to select the types of files you want to have backed up. You can choose from an extensive list of data file types, as shown in Fig. 6.14. There's even an **Additional Files** option you can choose for any data files not falling into the predefined categories. Select the file types you want to include in the backup and click the **Next** button.

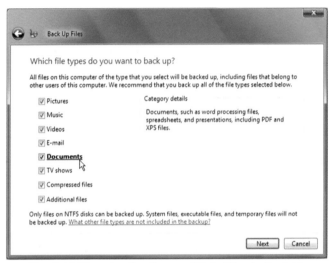

Fig. 6.14 Choosing the Types of Data Files to Back Up

In the next window (Fig. 6.15) you are asked how often you want backups to be automatically carried out, which can be daily, weekly of monthly. The first time you do this, Vista carries out a full backup of your data files, later scheduled backups will only include new, or modified, files. Choose the settings you want and click the **Save settings and start backup** button.

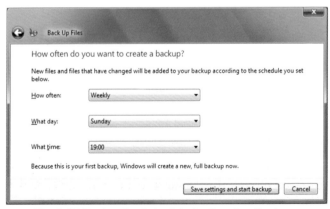

Fig. 6.15 Setting the Schedule for Creating Backups

The backup process then starts. First it will make a shadow copy, then it will scan the selected drives for files and folders and then it will create your backup. This can take some time, depending on your system and on how much data is being backed up. Our first full backup took over 5 hours! Subsequent ones though usually take from a few minutes up to an hour. This is no problem though, as you can carry on working during the process. You can stop a backup at any time by clicking the **Stop backup** button.

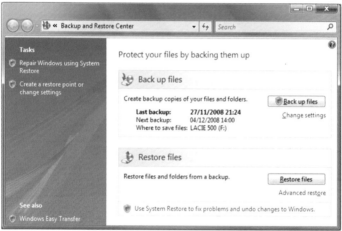

Fig. 6.16 Details of the Last and Next Scheduled Backups

Subsequent Backups

Once you create the initial backup, you really never have to think about backing up your files again since the **Back Up Files** wizard will regularly do this for you according to the schedule you set.

When you make a full backup, as described above, a backup folder is created and labelled with the date for that day. As updates are subsequently added with scheduled backups, they are placed in that folder and the date stays the same. The next time you make a full backup, a new backup folder is created and labelled with the new date, and any updates are then added to that new folder. You can then delete the older backup folder to save disc space.

Restoring from Backups

Restoring files and folders from your backups is not difficult, but is not an intuitive process either. You do it from the **Backup and Restore Center**, shown in Fig. 6.16 on the previous page, and most easily opened by clicking the **Start** button ⬤, typing **backup** in the search field, and selecting **Backup and Restore Center** from the list of results.

Clicking the **Advanced restore** option is used to restore an older backup that is not listed, or to carry out a complete restore operation. Unless your data has been seriously trashed, you would normally click the **Restore Files** button to start the procedure for restoring specific files and folders from the last backup. This opens the **Restore Files** wizard.

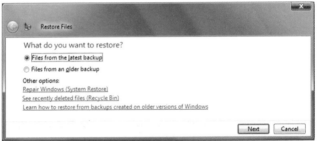

Fig. 6.17 The First Restore Files Dialogue Box

Select whether you want to restore files from the latest or an older backup, and click the **Next** button to continue.

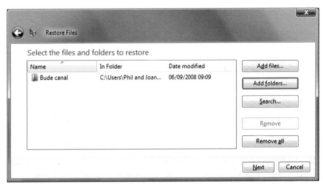

Fig. 6.18 The Second Restore Files Dialogue Box

In the second box (Fig. 6.18) you select the files or folders you want to restore, by clicking the **Add files** or **Add folders** buttons and selecting them from the standard Vista window that opens, like that shown in Fig. 6.19 below.

Fig. 6.19 Selecting the Files and Folders to Restore

You can also **Search** for a specific file if you know its name. When you have selected what you want to restore, click the **Next** button to continue.

Fig. 6.20 The Third Restore Files Dialogue Box

Select where you want to restore the files to (Fig. 6.20). You would normally pick to restore them to their original location, unless you want them somewhere else of course. Finally click the **Start Restore** button and watch the progress bar.

When the restore is completed, you will be told, and all you have to do then is click the **Finish** button.

You carry out a full restore from the **Backup Status and Configuration** window, which opens when you select the **Advanced restore** option shown in Fig. 6.16.

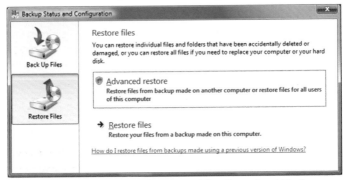

Fig. 6.21 The Backup Status and Configuration Window

To do this, click on **Advanced restore** (highlighted above) and select whether you want to restore from the latest backup, an older one, or one made on another PC. In the next window, tick the **Restore everything in this backup** check box, as shown in Fig. 6.22, click **Next** and carry on as in the previous example.

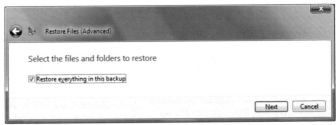

Fig. 6.22 Restoring Everything from a Backup

We are very impressed with Vista's backup and restore facilities. They are easy to use, and once you have set a procedure in motion you can forget it, safe in the knowledge that your data files are being regularly protected. Don't forget to do a complete backup every few months though!

7

The Control Panel

 The main way to control your PC is from the **Control Panel**, which provides quick and easy ways to change the hardware and software settings of your system.

To access the **Control Panel**, click the **Start** button ⚫, then left-click the **Control Panel** button on the black menu, as pointed to in Fig. 7.1 below.

Fig. 7.1 Opening the Control Panel

This opens the Control Panel window which can be viewed in two ways. The default, or Home view, as shown in Fig. 7.2, or in the Classic view as shown in Fig. 7.4.

To see the **Control Panel** in Classic view, left-click the **Classic View** link on the left panel (Fig. 7.2). To see it in the default view, click the **Control Panel Home** link. Which view you choose to work with is a matter of personal preference.

From either of these views, you can add new hardware, remove or change programs, change the display type and its resolution, change the printer fonts, change the size of the screen font, and change the keyboard repeat rate, etc. In other words you can set up Vista just how you want it.

Fig. 7.2 The Control Panel in the Default Vista View

Each option in the default view, shown above, has a listing below it of options relevant to that category. It is still not always easy to find what you want in the **Control Panel**, but don't forget that like most Vista windows, it has a **Search** box at the top. In Fig. 7.3 we typed **deaf** in the **Search** box and what we needed immediately appeared below. This is cool.

Fig. 7.3 Control Panel Search Results

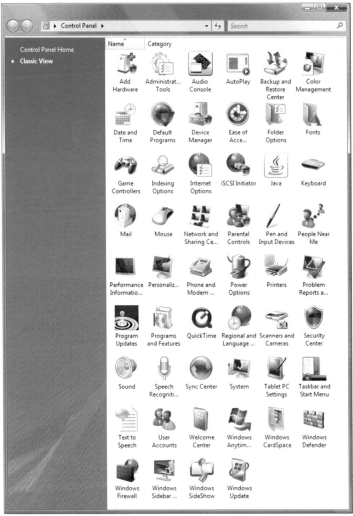

Fig. 7.4 The Control Panel in Classic View

All of the features in the **Control Panel** let you easily control the environment in which the Vista application programs operate, so it's a very good idea to become familiar with them. Just click on the links and see what is available.

Changing your Display

The 3D aspects of Vista require the highest possible screen resolution that your graphics card is capable of delivering. Higher screen resolution gives you better text clarity, sharper images, and more items fit on your screen, in other words you can see more. At lower resolutions, less items fit on the screen, and images may appear with jagged edges.

For example, a display resolution of 800 × 600 pixels (picture elements) is low, while one of 1600 × 1200 pixels is high. In general, LCD monitors can support higher resolutions than CRT monitors and whether you can increase your screen resolution depends on the size and capability of your monitor and the type of video card installed in your computer.

To find out if you can increase the display resolution of your computer screen, try the following:

In the **Control Panel** window (Fig. 7.2), click the **Adjust screen resolution** link, in the **Appearance and Personalization** section to open the Display Settings box.

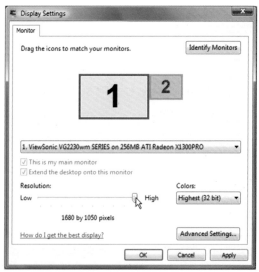

Fig. 7.5 The Display Settings Box

In this box, drag the resolution slider towards **High**, as shown in Fig. 7.5 on the facing page. Does it look any better? If so, for the new settings to take effect, click the **Apply** button, then click **OK** to close the window.

Next, click the **Appearance and Personalization** option itself in the Control Panel, to open the window in Fig. 7.6.

Fig. 7.6 The Appearance and Personalization Options

Plenty to explore here. Why don't you try the following:

Click the **Change desktop background** link to change the background of your Desktop, as in Fig. 7.7. In the **Location** list the three to look at first are **Windows Wallpapers**, **Sample Pictures** and **Solid Colours**. Or you can **Browse** your hard disc to find one of your own photos to use. Have a look at the positioning options at the bottom.

If you use one of your own photos and use the **Fit to screen** positioning, it will look better if you can crop its size to the same shape as your screen. You can do this in the Windows Photo Gallery with the **Fix**, **Crop Picture** commands and choose the right **Proportion** setting.

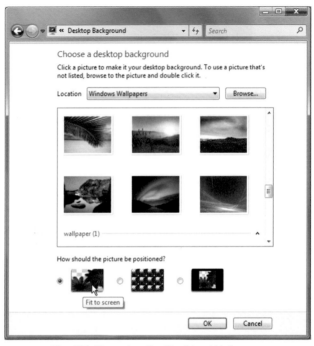

Fig. 7.7 Changing the Desktop Wallpaper

Use the **Back to Control Panel** button ⊙ and click the **Change screen saver** link to select a different screen saver (Fig. 7.8). You will be able to preview your selection before making a final choice.

Fig. 7.8 Changing the Screen Saver

Changing the Font Size of Screen Items

Since increasing screen resolution makes items appear smaller on the screen, you might well need a way of increasing the size of text and icons on the screen without compromising their clarity and resolution.

To do this, open the **Control Panel**, and click the **Appearance and Personalization** option to display the window shown earlier in Fig. 7.6. Click the **Personalization** link in this window to open the window shown in Fig. 1.13 on page 9.

On the left panel of the screen, click the **Adjust font size (DPI)** link and open the DPI Scaling dialogue box shown in Fig. 7.9 below. Select the **Larger scale (120 DPI)** option and click **Apply**. You will be warned to save all your work before restarting Windows, for the effect to take place. If you don't like it, go through the procedure again, but choose the **Default** option.

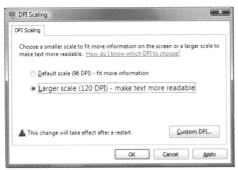

Fig. 7.9 Using DPI Scaling to Change Screen Font Size

Fig. 7.10 Custom Settings

If you click the **Custom DPI** button the customising dialogue box shown in Fig. 7.10 opens. This lets you experiment with different font scalings from a drop-down percentage menu and a slider bar. You should be able to find the setting you want.

Controlling Printers

When your Vista computer was first set up, your printers should have been installed automatically. If not, select **Printer** in the **Hardware and Sound** section of the **Control Panel**, or click the **Start** button ⬤ and choose **Printers** from the right column of the **Start** menu. Both of these open the **Printers** folder, shown in Fig. 7.11 below.

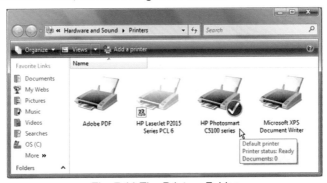

Fig. 7.11 The Printers Folder

Our **Printers** folder has several printers available as shown above. Two physical ones for printing to paper and two for creating formatted print documents **(.pdf** and **.xps)**.

With Vista, most printers are automatically detected at installation time, or during the boot-up process. This is called **Plug and Play**. So if you add a new printer to your system it should be recognised by Vista. You may be asked for the necessary driver files if they are not already in the Windows directory, but these normally come on a CD with a new printer anyway. If not, you can usually find them on the printer manufacturer's Web site.

If you are unlucky and your printer is not Plug and Play, the **Add a Printer** toolbar button 🖳 Add a printer provides a way of adding it. Clicking it, opens the Add Printer box which steps you through the process of adding both local printers (attached to your PC) and ones on your network. Again, you will need up-to-date driver files from a CD or the Web.

Configuring your Printer

To configure your printer, right-click its icon in the **Printers** folder (Fig. 7.11), and select the **Properties** option to open the Properties dialogue box for the selected printer.

Fig. 7.12 The Printer Properties Box

Here you can control all the printer's parameters, such as the printer port (or network path), paper and graphics options, built-in fonts, and other device options specific to the printer.

After you've added a printer, you can make sure it is working correctly by clicking the **Print Test Page** button. A newly installed printer is automatically set as the default printer, indicated by a green tick 🟢 against it in the **Printers** folder. To change this, select a printer connected to your PC, right-click it, and choose the **Set as Default Printer** option.

Once you have installed and configured your printers in Vista the quickest way to print a simple document or file is to print using Vista itself. Locate the file that you want to print in a folder, maybe **Documents**, right-click it, and select **Print**. Vista will print it using your default printer settings. How easy can that be? You don't even need to open the file, choose print options, or change printer settings.

For more control of the print operation, you should open the document in the program used to create it, and use its **File**, **Print** menu options.

Managing Print Jobs

If you want to find out what is happening when you have sent documents to your printer, double-click the printer that you are using in the **Printers** folder, or if something is actually printing, double-click the printer icon 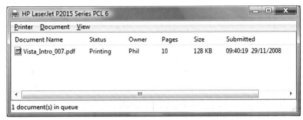 in the Notification Area of the Taskbar, to open the **Print Queue**.

Fig. 7.13 The Print Queue

This displays detailed information about the work actually being printed, or of print jobs that are waiting in the queue. This includes the name of the document, its status and 'owner', when it was added to the print queue, the printing progress and when printing was started.

   You can control the printing operations from the **Printer** and **Document** menu options of the **Print Queue** window. Selecting **Printer**, **Pause Printing** will stop the operation until you make the same selection again. The **Cancel All Documents** option will remove all the print jobs from the queue, but it sometimes takes a while.

Adding Hardware to your System

Vista automates the process of adding hardware (printers, scanners, monitors, mice, etc.) to your system by supporting what are known as Plug-and-Play devices. You just plug these into your computer and let Windows automatically install the driver software. So, when you buy new hardware, make sure that it is Plug-and-Play compatible. Adding such hardware devices to your system is extremely easy, as Windows takes charge and automatically controls all its settings so that it fits in with the rest of the system.

Add New Hardware Wizard – If your new hardware is not Plug-and-Play compatible all is not lost, as Vista has a very powerful Wizard which should help you with the installation. Fit the new hardware before you run the Wizard, as it is just possible that Windows will recognise the change and be able to carry out the configuration by itself.

You start the wizard from the Classic view of the **Control Panel**, opened by left-clicking the **Classic View** link on the left panel of the Default, or Home, view.

Double-clicking the **Add Hardware** icon, shown here, starts the Wizard which searches your system for anything new. If the new hardware is not recognised, a list of hardware is displayed and you are asked to specify its type. Good luck.

Fig. 7.14 Starting the Add Hardware Wizard

Working with Programs

Installing programs on your PC is very easy with Vista. Just place the CD or DVD that the software came on in the appropriate drive and Vista will start the installation process automatically. If you downloaded the program from the Internet, it should run and install itself.

Clicking the **Programs** section of the **Control Panel** opens the sub-panel shown in Fig. 7.15.

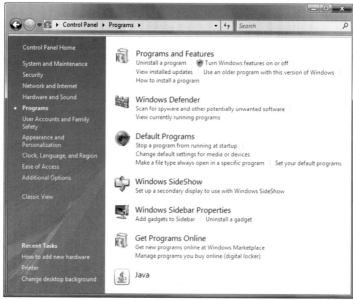

Fig. 7.15 The Programs Section of the Control Panel

Uninstall or Change a Program

Uninstalling programs or changing an already installed one is very easy with Vista. To do either, click the **Uninstall a program** link in the **Programs and Features** section of the **Control Panel**, shown in Fig. 7.15 above, to open a very colourful screen similar to the one in Fig. 7.16. Your contents will not be the same, obviously!

Fig. 7.16 Uninstalling and Changing Programs

After selecting a program the four options, **Organize**, **Views**, **Uninstall**, and **Change** may appear on the toolbar, as shown above. With some programs **Change** is not available, while with others it is replaced by the **Repair** option.

Using the option to **Uninstall** a program, removes all trace of it from your hard disc, although sometimes the folders are left empty on your hard drive.

Note: Be careful with this application, because double-clicking a program on the list may well remove it without further warning!

Windows Features

Some programs and features that are included with Windows Vista, must be turned on before you can use them. Other features are turned on by default, but you can turn them off if you don't need them.

You probably won't need to make any changes here, but if you do, just click the **Turn Windows features on or off** link, shown in the left panel of Fig. 7.16, and select the features you want included with Vista, as shown below.

Fig. 7.17 Turning Windows features On or Off

We have only managed to cover a fraction of the features and controls available in the Vista **Control Panel**. Over time, maybe you will explore the rest, with the help of the **Search** boxes at the top of most folders and windows.

8

Accessibility

Ease of
Access
Center

Vista's **Ease of Access Center**, located in the **Control Panel**, lets you change settings to make your PC more accessible for people who have visual difficulties, hearing loss, pain in their hands or arms, or reasoning and cognitive issues.

To see it, open the **Control Panel** by clicking the **Start** button ⊙ followed by the **Control Panel** link. Click the **Classic View** link so that all the available utilities are visible (see Fig. 7.4), and then double-click the **Ease of Access Center** button, shown above. An easier way is just to use the ⊞+U keyboard shortcut. Both methods open the window shown in Fig. 8.1 on the next page.

The **Ease of Access Center** includes a quick access panel at the top with a highlight rotating through the four most common tools; **Magnifier**, **Narrator**, **On-Screen Keyboard**, and **High Contrast**. A voice, the Narrator, also tells you what option is selected. Pressing the **Spacebar** on a highlighted option will start it for you.

If the Narrator annoys you, click the **Always read this section aloud** box to remove the tick mark from it. While you are doing this, you could also remove the tick mark from the **Always scan this section** box, to stop the focus from rotating between the four entries.

The **Get recommendations...** link opens a five-stage questionnaire. Depending on your answers to questions about performing routine tasks, such as whether you have difficulty seeing faces or text on TV, hearing conversations, or using a pen or pencil, Vista will provide a recommendation of the accessibility settings and programs that are likely to improve your ability to see, hear, and use your computer. This has to be a good place to start.

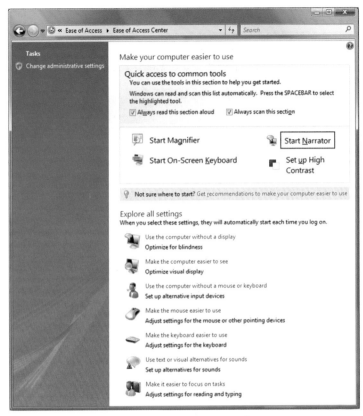

Fig. 8.1 The Ease of Access Center

The **Explore all settings** section at the bottom of the **Ease of Access Center** lets you explore settings options by categories. When selected, these will automatically start each time you log on to the computer.

They include; using the computer without a display, making the computer easier to see, using the computer without a mouse or keyboard, changing mouse or keyboard settings, using text or visual alternatives for sounds, and making it easier to focus on tasks.

The Microsoft Magnifier

To start the Magnifier, click on **Start Magnifier** (words not icon) situated in the middle of the window shown in Fig. 8.1.

Fig. 8.2 Computer Screen with the Magnifier Active

A new Magnifier window is placed at the top of the screen as shown in Fig. 8.2 above. Wherever you place the mouse

pointer on the actual (lower) screen, is shown magnified in the upper window at the top of the screen. You can make the Magnifier window bigger by clicking it, then moving the pointer to the lower edge of the window until it changes to a four-headed arrow and dragging the edge down.

Clicking the **Magnifier** icon on the **Taskbar**, opens the Magnifier box shown in Fig. 8.3.

Fig. 8.3 The Magnifier Control Box

From here you can set the **Scale factor** from 1 (low) to 16 (high), select other **Presentation** options, such as the docking position of the Magnifier window, and set **Tracking** options.

Selecting **Minimize on Startup** under **Option**, minimises the **Magnifier** on the **Taskbar** next time you start the application. To close the **Magnifier**, click its entry on the **Taskbar** and click the **Close** button [▬X▬].

Microsoft Narrator

Narrator is a basic screen reader built into Vista and may be useful for the visually impaired. It reads dialogue boxes and window controls in a number of Windows basic applications, as long as the computer being used has a sound card and speakers or headphones.

Fig. 8.4 Microsoft Narrator

To open it, click the **Start Narrator** option in the **Ease of Access Center** (Fig. 8.1). Anna will start speaking in an electronic voice and the Microsoft Narrator window will open, as shown in Fig. 8.4. This is where you can customise and control the **Narrator**.

Clicking on **Voice Settings** lets you set the talking speed, volume and pitch. There is an option to change the voice, but our system only seemed to have the default 'Microsoft Anna'.

If you find this facility useful you will need to play around with the **Main Narrator Settings** until you get it working the best way for you. It may also be a good time to think about getting a full-function screen reader to make your general computing a little more enjoyable.

To close **Narrator** just click the **Exit** button.

The On-Screen Keyboard

To activate the **On-Screen Keyboard** (Fig. 8.5), click the **Start On-Screen Keyboard** option in the **Ease of Access Center** shown earlier in Fig. 8.1.

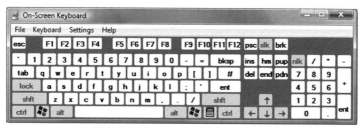

Fig. 8.5 The On-Screen Keyboard

The virtual keyboard allows users with mobility impairments to type data using a mouse pointer, a joystick, or other pointing device. The result is exactly as if you were using the actual keyboard.

The **On-Screen Keyboard** has three typing modes you can use to type data. These are:

Clicking mode – you click the on-screen keys to type text.

Hovering mode – you use a mouse or joystick to point to a key for a predefined period of time, and the selected character is typed automatically.

Scanning mode – the **On-Screen Keyboard** continually scans the keyboard and highlights areas where you can type keyboard characters by pressing a hot key or using a switch-input device.

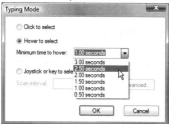

These typing modes are selected by choosing the **Settings**, **Typing Mode** menu command to open the Typing Mode dialogue box shown in Fig. 8.6.

Fig. 8.6 Setting the Typing Mode

You can also select from the **Settings** menu to have the virtual keyboard appear **Always on Top** of all other windows displayed on your screen, and also select to **Use Click Sound** which is particularly useful if you are using the **Hover to select** option of **Typing Mode**.

There are several types of **On-Screen Keyboards** available from the **Keyboard** menu. These are:

Enhanced Keyboard with the numeric keypad.

Standard Keyboard without the numeric keypad.

You can also display the keyboard with the keys in the **Regular Layout**, or in a **Block Layout** (arranged in rectangular blocks). **Block Layout** is especially useful in scanning mode. Finally, you can select to display the US standard keyboard (**101 keys**), the universal keyboard (**102 keys**), or a keyboard with additional Japanese language characters (**106 keys**).

Keyboard Options

If you have trouble using the actual keyboard, you may like to click the **Make the keyboard easier to use** link in the **Ease of Access Center** shown in Fig. 8.1. This opens the window shown in Fig. 8.7 on the next page. From here you can tick the **Turn on Sticky Keys** option, which allows you to press the **Ctrl**, **Alt**, and **Shift**, keys one at a time, instead of all at the same time. This is useful for people who have difficulty pressing two or more keys at a time.

The **Turn on Filter Keys** option (Fig. 8.7), tells the keyboard to ignore brief or repeated keystrokes. The keyboard repeat rate can also be adjusted here.

If you activate the **Turn on Toggle Keys** option (Fig. 8.7), your PC will play a high-pitched sound when the **Caps Lock**, **Scroll Lock**, or **Num Lock** keys are used.

The **Set up...** links against each of the above options allow for fine tuning of these preferences.

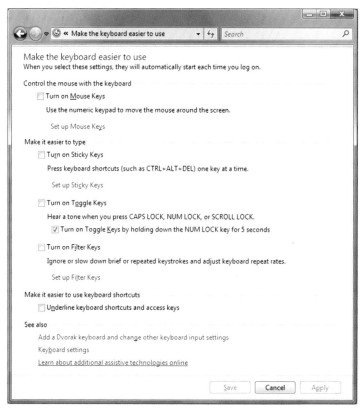

Fig. 8.7 Making the Keyboard Easier to Use

The **Turn on Mouse Keys** option can also be enabled here, which lets you move the mouse pointer by pressing the arrow (cursor) keys on the keyboard's numeric pad.

You should be careful with some of the Accessibility options, as once they are selected they will start automatically every time your computer is switched on. Getting rid of them can sometimes be a problem.

With this in mind, perhaps it would be a good idea to set a new **System Restore** point before making too many changes (see page 79).

Alternatives for Sounds

Clicking the **Use text or visual alternatives for sounds** link in Fig. 8.1 displays the window in Fig. 8.8 below, in which you can instruct your PC to flash part of its screen every time the system's built-in speaker plays a sound. In addition, you can choose which part of the screen you want to flash.

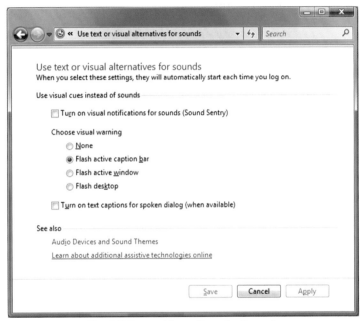

Fig. 8.8 Some Alternatives for Sounds

The Display Options

Activating the **Set up High Contrast** option in Fig. 8.1, opens the window shown in Fig. 8.9 on the next page. Here you can set programs to change their colour-specific schemes to a **High Contrast** scheme specified by you. Fonts can also be changed whenever possible to improve legibility.

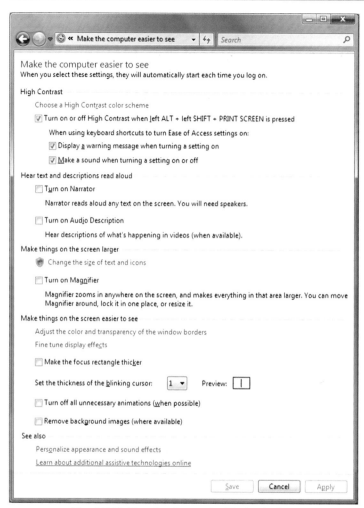

Fig. 8.9 Making the Computer Easier to See

You can also change the rate at which the insertion point blinks and its width by dragging the two sliders appropriately. This window has a good selection of visibility options to explore.

The Mouse Options

Activating the **Make the mouse easier to use** link in Fig. 8.1, displays the window below.

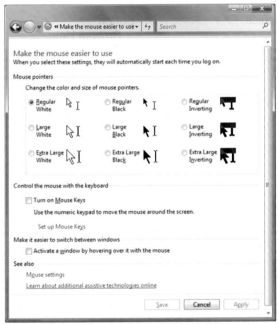

Fig. 8.10 Making the Mouse Easier to Use

Here you can change the colour and size of the mouse pointer, and control the mouse pointer's movements with the keys on the numeric keypad.

Clicking the **Set up Mouse Keys** link, displays an additional window in which you can control, amongst other things, the speed at which the mouse pointer moves, and the shortcut key combination you need to activate and deactivate the numeric keypad.

Index